Praise for *A Rescued Life*

"Tamela Turbeville is one of the best storytellers I've had the pleasure of coaching. It may have taken her forty years to believe her story mattered, but it is because of her reluctance that makes you trust her all the more. Let Tamela help take you through the process of removing your secrets of shame to find freedom, hope, and healing to believe your story matters (because it does)."

—**Renee Fisher,** Life Coach and Author of
Forgiving Others, Forgiving Me

"*A Rescued Life* is a gift for every person who has been wounded by the brokenness of our world. Tamela uses poignant imagery and captivating details to offer hope and healing as she shares the difficult, shameful, and traumatic parts of her own story. If you're ready to find healing from your past, claim victory over shame, and uncover hope in your heartache, this book is a must-read for you."

—**Stacey Pardoe,** author of *Flourish in the Fire* and
founder of *Encountering God in the Ordinary*

"I am so thankful for Tamela's honest sharing of her story. Through her transparency and Christ-centeredness, she has offered readers an opportunity to reflect on the mercy and goodness of the Lord in their own journeys!"

—**Ann Swindell,** author of *Still Waiting: Hope for
When God Doesn't Give You What You Want*

"In her book *A Rescued Life*, Tamela tells the story of a world where she felt worthless and the God who pursued and rescued her. This story shines light through the cracks, the places where we are broken, and radiates hope. You cannot put this book down without first grabbing hold of a handful of feel-good affirmation of your worth to a God who pursues and rescues the lost girl in each of us."

—**Laurie Hampton,** Beautifully Broken
(www.lauriehampton.com)

"'For the wages of sin is death, but the free gift of God is eternal life in Christ Jesus our Lord.' The first half of Romans 6:23 explains our problem (the problem we ALL have) and the second half explains God's rescue plan (His plan for ALL of us). God's perfect rescue plan runs through the entire Bible. In *A Rescued Life*, Tamela shares openly and transparently about her Romans 6:23a-life. She proves "the wages of sin is death" to be true. And then...God's rescue plan unfolded. He rescued her! He alone rescues! Tamela shows us why Jesus came and suffered in an evil, evil world. Why? To rescue us. And praise God, His gift is both free and eternal!"

—**Debbie Moore,** Arkansas Baptist State Convention,
Missions Team/Consultant, Arkansas WMU
Executive Director

"Enter a typical school classroom and know that one or more of the youngsters seated there will have suffered childhood sexual abuse. Writer Tamela Turbeville transforms statistics into stark reality in the brave and harrowing tale of abuse in her own early life, as well as the effects she lived with for years. Her recovery is not a quick fix. It unfolds over decades. She generously takes her audience through many traumatic years and missteps to a resolution that is realistic and inspiring. This is a brave book. Readers will find both realism and hope in Tamela Turbeville's superb story."

—**Dr. Toran Isom,** Writing Faculty Emeritus,
University of Arkansas—Little Rock, Department of
Rhetoric and Writing

"Statistically, one in six women in the United States experience sexual abuse/assault. This creates a trauma that goes to the very core of a woman's soul and can negatively impact every area of her life. Scripture tells us to "lay aside every weight, and sin which clings so closely, and let us run with endurance the race that is set before us" (Hebrews 12:1b, ESV). The past sixteen years of working in women's ministry have taught me that the greatest weight women carry is the trauma of sexual abuse. I am so grateful for Tamela revealing her journey to spiritual freedom. It is my prayer that through her transparency and incredible courage, women will realize they are not alone and seek out Christian help."

—**Debra K. Burchfield,** CEO, Hope of the Delta

Published by Living Rescued, LLC

208 Elizabeth Ann Drive

White Hall, AR 71602

Cover & Interior Layout Design by Nelly Murariu at PixBeeDesign.com

978-0-578-84631-6 Paperback
978-0-578-84632-3 eBook

Library of Congress Control Number: 2021907830

A Rescued Life

A Story of Secrets and Shame, Hope and Healing

TAMELA TURBEVILLE

You are stronger than you think – Blessings, Tamela Turbeville

Dedication

To God.
You gave me this story to tell.

To my sons, Ian, Kyle, and Ryan.
I love you more than you will know.
You are the reason I can tell this story.

Contents

Foreword

I have had the sacred opportunity to journey alongside some of the bravest people on the planet. While many adventurers may daringly step into places unknown, only the bravest of souls will willfully choose to trek into places of the past to face the traumatic memories of childhood. I have been privileged to witness firsthand the seeds of healing that grow along this journey and the chains of shame that are broken along the path to freedom. To be trusted as a guide on this sacred journey is a considerable honor, but the greatest joy of all is watching as a brave, yet fearful soul becomes the hero his or her story needs.

It was through Tamela's determination and fight that she became the rescuer in her story for the little girl whose voice was taken, leaving her feeling forever lost. This act of rescue allowed her to discover how loveable and worthy she has always been and how God was faithful to pursue His beloved. Week after week, I was an audience to how God was healing her as she was learning to embrace her bravery and strength. We often ended sessions in prayer and the reminder, "You are stronger than you think you are."

You are also stronger than you think you are. Like with Tamela, encouragement and support from another can motivate you to take the next step toward healing. The internal dialog that you listen to also has a great impact on the steps you take. For instance, there is a big difference between the voice of conviction and the voice of shame. The voice of conviction sounds like those precious words Tamela heard say, "Try counseling." Too often, the voice of conviction is drowned out by the lies from the all-too-familiar voice of shame. What does that voice of conviction sound like for you? What about the voice of hope? The wise words you need to hear may very well be found in the encouragement you have offered a friend. You, likewise, deserve the same compassion.

This memoir was years in the making and beautifully scripted out of true healing that comes from our Heavenly Father. Every page points to God's amazing love for those who have suffered and lost. Join Tamela on this journey to find the freedom that you were created to know and experience.

—**April,** Licensed Professional Counselor*

Introduction: Why Tell This Story?

Keeping a secret has been called an "obsession in a jar." A secret will not go away. Depending on the type of secret, the more you try to hide it, the more you think about it. The more you think about it, the more that secret leads your life. The more potent the secret, the more damage it creates. Compound a potent secret with the unnecessary shame of rape or sexual assault, and that secret can be terminal.

Statistically, one in six women are victims of sexual abuse or assault, most often as children.[1] I know from experience that this statistic is accurate, and most of you know it is true as well. You either have experienced the pain of abuse or know someone who has.

Until the most recent decade, sexual abuse of any kind was a taboo topic. When I was growing up, the subject was not mentioned—anywhere. There was no yearly awareness campaign or speeches made by the high school counselor. If it happened to you, you kept it a secret. So, I did.

At the time I suffered sexual abuse—during the 1970s—awareness was just being born and would not be fully grown until after I suffered for forty years from the shame that was not mine. When it happened to me, it was decades before the #MeToo movement would arrive and give sexually assaulted women the voice and strength to tell their secret. I applaud and offer my gratitude to the women who courageously paved the way for women like me to tell their stories.

Before it was acceptable to talk about sexual assault, during the "between" years, I lived under the heavy weight of the secret and shame. When the #MeToo movement finally arrived, the damage was done. The secrets and shame led to a whole list of destructive choices and a life of sin. The years between the secret made and the secret told were dark years for me.

I did not understand what was happening. I did not link the past to the present. I did not see that the shame given me by a teenage boy one summer afternoon was not mine, yet I carried it through decades of fear, depression, addiction, and so much more. The secret and the shame changed who I was and who I would become.

I believed I would never tell. I believed if I told the secret no one would love me, want me, or even believe me. Which is ironic, because I believed at the same time that I was unlovable, unwanted, and not worth noticing even if I kept the secret. I was unlovable if I told and unlovable if I didn't. It was a double-edged secret.

But when I exposed the secret to light, just the opposite happened. Telling the secret saved me. It freed me to see that God loves me, God was and is with me, and God fights for me. I believe He rescued me so I could tell the story of my secret and shame and share how telling leads to healing and hope.

I believe
He rescued me so
I could tell the story
of my secret and
shame and share
how telling
leads to healing
and hope.

This rescue story has been nearly sixty years in the making. If the enemy had his way, it never would have been started.

There were obstacles upon obstacles that he threw in my path to deter God's plan. I should have given up years ago and let it go, but I could not. I must tell about the great things He has done for me (Psalm 22:22).

If I look back at my teenage years, I see the little girl harmed by rape, and then just years later God placed a desire and a dream in her to write. See how the two were lining up? It would be over forty years before the lines converged, but they did. In between, that same girl would live under the control of shame, not the love of God. Choices would be guided by shame, not freedom.

Eventually, I pursued writing and completed an undergraduate and a master's degree in writing. In the meantime, God wove together a story of secrets and shame knowing I would be rescued at just the right time, and at the exact perfect moment I would be able to write this story. He designed a life of secrets and shame that would be redeemed by hope and healing. Then, He gave me the opportunity to share it with the world.

I did not want to write this story as a memoir. When I knew God called me to write this story, I began like most novice writers, copying other writers. I wanted a Beth Moore-like Bible study and to use my story to illustrate biblical concepts. It did not work. In fact, it was awful. It was painful to write and even more painful to read!

Not until my gifted and God-sent dream defender, Renee Fisher, suggested I remove the "preaching" did the story finally flow. God is still there in the story. There is no way my story is redeemed without His presence and grace. I did nothing remarkable to reach freedom from secrets and shame and begin healing from sexual assault. No, it was all God. So, I guess that is the Bible lesson.

If you are one of the thousands of women who suffered sexual abuse of any kind and feel there is no way out of the shame prison, there is. Don't wait another day carrying shame that is not yours. Bring the secret out into the light. Compassionate counselors, survivors, and a host of other people are ready and poised to help.

So many of us have secrets. Your secret may not be abuse. Perhaps it's abortion, addiction, or adultery. And because of that secret you feel the heavy weight of shame. There is relief. There is freedom from your shame prison. There is God. You don't have to carry the secret or shame another day.

God is waiting to rescue you.

CHAPTER 1

Forty Years Later

A Storm

Outside, I hear the sweetest summer thunderstorm rumbling through. Lightning flashes, thunderclaps roll, and sheets of torrential rain blow sideways. Out my window the weather rages and, oddly, I find it comforting, not only because I am safe, warm, and dry. I find it reassuring because I know the chaotic storm will blow over, and the earth and my garden will be better for its brief presence. In the meantime, it will be noisy, and sometimes scary, but if I hang on, and persevere, it will stop, and on the other side is peace. I learned this truth by surviving some pretty tumultuous storms.

Storms are born when two opposing forces collide. A cold and warm front smash together in the atmosphere, and with the right amount of moisture, the sky explodes. Friction between the two forces creates lightning. Then, the lightning heats the air as it heads toward the earth, causing startling thunderclaps that travel miles before disintegrating. After the storm tires and the friction ceases, the storm is replaced by a restful peace.

The storms that erupt in our lives are the same. They form through opposing forces like good and evil, trust and betrayal, kindness and hate, the past and the present. These forces create friction that leads

1

to a lot of noise and disruption—and possibly damage—and then fade, leaving room for God's transforming, healing work to occur.

The tempests of life come in many forms, and their force depends on the circumstances that bring them about. Some storms can be seen brewing in the distance. For instance, tense relationships that cause harsh words or disagreements can cause smaller storms. These outbreaks come quickly, pour out emotions, and then subside, hopefully with minimal damage.

On other occasions, storms grow over time. These can be the result of ignoring a suffering marriage or rebellious children or the consequences of poor choices. These storms multiply and expand until they explode. Sometimes there is irreparable damage, and other times the explosion is needed to clear the air.

And yet other storms come out of nowhere. Unexpectedly, turmoil bursts forth. These emotional storms suddenly appear and cause unexpected heartache and pain. Perhaps these storms are the result of betrayal or broken trust, or a sudden illness or catastrophy. The destruction can take a lifetime to heal. This kind of storm swirls into a hurricane.

Some storms are quickly forgotten. Others, like a hurricane, linger in our memory and change the course of our lives. One such out-of-the-blue, hurricane-force storm I cannot forget. It crashed through my typical Monday five years back. Through grace, I was rescued and survived, but this storm changed the course of my life.

I was sitting in my car waiting for my youngest son to emerge from the high school building. I was scrolling through my Facebook feed, and suddenly his face was staring back at me. Boom, the thunder clapped and the lightning struck. A storm was born.

The "People You Might Know" category caught me completely off guard, because I did know him. It was him, that boy—now an old man. He looked right at me through the screen. I was unable to move or look away. His face was staring at me, and he was doing it with a half-smirk on his lips.

The hurricane blew me sideways.

In a split second, some cosmic power grabbed me around the shoulders and in lighting speed thrust me back forty years. My peripheral vision blurred, and in a blink, it was summer 1974. I was an eleven-year-old girl with pigtails tied tight on opposite sides of my blonde head. My skinny suntanned legs were sticking out of a pair of jean shorts, and I leaned on the seat of a pink bicycle, resplendent with fringe on the handlebars and a white basket. The memory was so clear, I could smell the summer air and the scent of sweaty boys when they stood close together, laughing and punching each other on the arm.

The air left my lungs, and my chest grew too tight for me to take in a breath. Frozen, my eyes would not look away. It was like I was watching myself from the back seat of the car and everything was moving in slow motion.

Staring at the screen on my phone, I was trapped in the past. I had tried to forget this face for decades. But there it was looking at me—the boy who raped me.

After what seemed like hours of swirling around in the past in my head, my personal hurricane began to calm. I heard a ringing noise in my ears. I faintly made out a voice. "Mom, are you okay? Mom, what's wrong?" My son was shaking my arm, bringing me back from the past. And as quickly as the universe shot into the past four decades, it boomeranged back to reality.

An hour after I returned home from the high school, I was curled up in bed with the covers pulled over my head. I sobbed until my pillow dripped, and I prayed my family could not hear me. I was reliving that day from forty years ago and felt the shame so heavy I wanted to crawl on my hands and knees. I tried so hard to bury the memory of that summer day and forget his face. Obviously, I was unsuccessful. It was not so deep that a photo on social media couldn't unearth it.

I ached to rid myself of this memory. I had tried everything, but that moment in time kept creeping up, this time with a face. I needed a new plan.

God has eyes on the tiniest sparrow blown off course by storms.

My first plan went something like this: take multiple pills, mix with alcohol, and sleep. I had tried variations of this plan in the past. Every attempt failed, of course. As with the previous attempts, I hoped that someone found me before I passed from this world to the next. Not living seemed like a better choice than living a day longer with the secret of what happened in 1974. But, thankfully—gratefully—God has eyes on the tiniest sparrow blown off course by storms. And this storm had me flailing in the wind.

I worked desperately hard every day of every year for over four decades to keep the secret this boy left me with under control. There were times I actually forgot the secret for a moment. I would bury it deep under shame and regret. Then something would remind me. Sometimes the smell of cigarettes or the sound of a cola bottle popping open would make me remember, but mostly I kept the secret out of sight.

There was a time that I tried to tell myself that the secret I kept for forty years wasn't real, that maybe it didn't happen the way I remembered. Perhaps I asked for it in some way. Maybe it was my fault. The eleven-year-old little girl could not make sense of it.

After the boy next door raped me, I was too afraid to tell anyone. What would they think of me? My mother and father would surely be so angry and embarrassed that I was their child. I tried to run from it, hide from it, escape it—but it always showed up in a flash of a memory, a smell, a word—and I would remember. I worked so hard to keep it under control, yet it escaped again and again. I was exhausted. My shame secret was chained to me, and there was no hope of escape. I had to do something drastic to unchain myself from this secret.

The next day, in my car, driving down the interstate, I was still formulating the plan. I cannot remember where I was going, but my destination sent me in the direction of a real storm forming on the horizon. Dark gray clouds multiplied in the distance, and I marveled at how they mirrored my mood—dark, rumbling, angry, and growing increasingly dangerous and about to explode. In no time, pouring rain pelted the windshield so hard the taillights of the car in front me were barely visible.

Before I carried out any plan I would finally formulate, I decided I would ask God for help. Isn't it funny how we go to God *after* we have a plan, not before? Isn't it odd how we ask God for help with *our* plans, not giving a second thought to His plan? Shame is so powerful that it assumes God doesn't like us either, that He made a mistake and He would be happy to help us end our pain. That is the lie we believe, and after a while, it becomes our truth.

Driving my SUV along the three-lane interstate in pouring rain, I begged through streams of tears, "Take me, please. I cannot live another day. I want to drown." Maybe I thought He would cause me to wreck my car, and my family would mourn my death caused by a car accident and not by my own hand. "Take me. Stop the pain. Please, take me," I pleaded. When I think about that afternoon now, I laugh at the absurdity of my words. I begged to end my pain forever while at the same time I knew God is the one in control.

"I have this plan, God, but I don't want to carry it out. Would you make something else happen?"

As audibly as I could hear the contemporary Christian music playing on the radio and the hail thumping the roof of my car, I heard God's voice. "Try counseling," a small gentle voice said. It seems so silly now—God suggesting a therapist. I would have thought I was crazy if the voice had not pierced my soul. The words of the voice sounded like the advice from a trusted friend yet filled with authority. This was the opposite of what I wanted to hear. In the middle of a storm raging around me and in me, I wanted something drastic, final, and easy. But God suggested I try a few Christian counseling sessions. It seemed so crazy it could not have been my voice.

When God speaks, we think it should sound like Charlton Heston and the words be more biblical, "Go, therefore, and see a counselor." No, it was more like a flash of clarity. There was no condemnation or scolding, just an overwhelming peace, the turmoil of my inner storm turned off like a water faucet.

Of one thing I was sure: it was not my idea. Counseling or telling anyone any detail of my childhood was not, absolutely not, on my radar. I was more willing to commit suicide than tell the secret. But God said to see a counselor, and I believe for the first time in my life, I obeyed. And because I did, God saved my life. He rescued me.

Wiping away the tears, pulling into an empty parking lot, and composing myself, I called the only person I knew who was both dependent on God and connected to Christian counselors. I knew my friend would know who to call, and she did.

We can't see when it's happening, but God always puts just the right people in our path at just the right time. My dear friend did not know it then, but she was an instrument of God's plan to save me. She gave me the phone number of a counseling service that could help, and when I ended our call, I dialed the number.

I asked for an appointment as soon as possible. The lead counselor was not available for months and not taking new clients. Maybe the receptionist heard the desperation in my voice, but she suggested the second counselor working in the office. Yes, I said without hesitation, I'll take it! I'll take the first appointment with any counselor. I was skeptical, but I would give God's plan a month. If it did not heal forty years of shame and secrets in thirty days, then I was going with my original plan—alcohol, drugs and a deep sleep. *You have one month, God, just one month.*

Broken

Once a week, usually on Wednesday afternoons, I spirited away to meet April.* I would learn in time that her counseling specialty is trauma more specifically abuse trauma. God knew exactly what I needed and who.

As each of our regular sessions drew near, I grew more and more excited. I was excited because our conversations opened a new door each week, removed another brick from the wall, and lightened my load of emotional rocks. I looked forward to our hours together, and I let nothing and no one get in the way. My life depended on being present at every appointment. And God only had thirty days.

I protected my time with April and sometimes may have treated our appointments as some kind of clandestine relationship. If someone asked about my plans for a midweek afternoon, I didn't hide that I was seeing a Christian counselor, but I also didn't share the information openly. Mostly because what usually followed my explanation was a combination of the awkward, uncomfortable phrases like, "That's great," and, "Everyone needs to see a counselor now and then." These were usually followed by a puzzled, anxious look that suggested they were thinking, *I wonder what's wrong with her?* Believe me, that is a deep ocean.

*Name has been changed to protect confidentiality.

If I did let it slip about my standing appointment with a therapist, and someone compassionately or curiously asked why I was seeing a counselor, I mumbled something vague about childhood issues. Nothing more would be asked. "Childhood issues" was broad enough to leave someone imagining all the possibilities but specific enough for them to realize the wound was deep. The inquiry always stopped there.

April's office was on the second floor of a local church's family life building, and, being too proud to use the elevator, I always climbed the two flights of stairs, reaching the top step out of breath and gasping for oxygen. For a counselor, she was not what I had expected. She would blush at my description, but she is young, with beautiful dark eyes and a soothing voice. April is a mom of school-aged kids, and their pictures were carefully and proudly positioned on her desk. Taking my place in her office once I caught my breath, I sat down on her white leather couch, replete with throw pillows, my gaze instantly fixed on the flame flickering in the fake electric fireplace directly opposite. The glow was hypnotic. She kept the room slightly dark, which was comforting and made it feel less clinical. There was no clock on the wall or desk—also comforting.

Time seemed to stop when she shut the door. I immediately felt safe, secure. I could let my guard down and relax. She always started our sessions with, "So, how was your week?" And, of course, I would start pouring out the details of the previous seven days. My husband did this; my kids did that. I enjoyed going to church so much. Or, I cried all day Saturday and couldn't get out of bed. Or, I ate an entire chocolate pie and felt better and worse at the same time. I realize her opening questions were ice breakers. It was a starting point, a place to jump from what was happening to what had happened.

I kept my promise. I gave God thirty days, and He was right. Seeing a counselor was helpful for the surface pain and turmoil. I embarrassingly admit that, for the first month, all I did was complain about what the world was doing to me. I complained about my marriage, how my husband didn't respect me, that he didn't hear me. I talked about how I felt like I was falling apart. I spoke of my mother, my father, and my childhood. *What a mess*, she must have been thinking, while at the same time wondering if I could be any more self-centered. I was a mess.

Breakthrough

During the first thirty days, April asked me to complete a timeline that included memorable events of my life from the day I was born through the present day. From top to bottom of a sheet of paper, I was to list every significant event of my fifty plus years on the left. On the right, I recorded how I was affected by the events. At the top, born December 1962. Not able to say how I felt about being born, but today, I am pleased with the outcome.

Several childhood memories listed on one side had left me stunned and broken. I recorded the day I ran away to New York City when I was eighteen. That was memorable! That event led to many distressful and shameful events in my twenties, creating more scars, of course. After I returned to my hometown five years later, other occasions left me ashamed and regretful as well. More on that later.

Not all of the events on the left side of the page left wounds. The birth of my first son was the day I learned how deep love goes. The moment I looked at his newborn eyes and perfect pink fingers and toes, my heart knew true unconditional love for the first time. Gratefully, that moment happened again a second and third time when second and third sons were born.

For a couple of months, during each appointment, April and I discussed the timeline and the major impactful events. I cried a lot and apologized for crying so much. I brought a personal box of tissues because I felt guilty for using so many of April's. April and I talked through my childhood and growing up in my family of origin. If nothing else, the most important lesson I learned was how deeply parents impact their children.

On one Wednesday, when we were slicing away at the timeline and reviewing the story of my life in the Big Apple, I shared something that I almost forgot. After five years of hard living, drinking, and promiscuity, I was at the bottom of the pit—twenty years old, no job, and barely a place to live. I was desperate and alone.

My family could not and would not help me. There was no place to turn. I was so ashamed of how I arrived at that point that I was sure God could not and would not help either. I was the prodigal daughter, running away from home, squandering every asset I possessed. God, I believed, must have abandoned me. Why not? When I looked in the mirror, I saw trash, and I believed He did, too.

When I looked in the mirror, I saw trash, and I believed He did, too.

My solution was to do what I had become good at—giving myself away. But now it would not be free. My excuse, "It's the only thing I was good at."

Poor April. If she was shocked, she never flinched. She smiled supportively and listened, and I knew she was not judging me. I was safe. I could keep going if I needed to, and I needed to. The room was silent for a moment. I needed more tissue, and I was afraid April needed to process the information. Then she asked, "Why do you think that's all you are worth?"

I knew the answer, but I had never, ever uttered the words. Not even come close. I believed my worth was tied to a secret. A secret never spoken, never written on paper, never hinted at in conversations. Never. To truly answer her question, I would have to tell the secret.

At first, it wouldn't come out. For more than forty years, the words were just under the surface, covered in layers of shame and regret, held down by fear. Here was the moment for exposing it to the light. The moment was right for fighting against the reins of shame.

The words crawled up my throat and out of my mouth like spiders. I could feel my tongue around the words I could never say. The sharp edges of the words ripped at my throat like they were trying to stay hidden. They wanted to crawl back to where they had lived for forty years. It was as if two forces were slamming up against each other. Darkness against light. The past against a possible future. Prison against freedom. Keep the secret versus let the secret go. Keep the secret. No, tell. Then, I heard the sound of thunder. Boom! I looked at the floor and blurted, "When I was eleven, I was raped."

April didn't blink. I was watching and waiting for her mouth to fall open in judgment and disgust as I feared people would do if they knew, but her compassion did not allow her to judge. Once the words left my mouth, the flood started, like a gate thrown open to let wild horses run into vast open spaces. There it was, at last, in the light. Not a secret anymore. And, of course, there were tears, buckets of tears. Rivers of tears. I cried oceans of tears in April's office, but on that day, they were tears of relief and mourning, relief from the chains of a forty-year-old shame secret and the mourning of the death of the past. Good thing I brought my own tissues.

Telling the secret came with both benefits and struggles. With more visits and tear-filled sessions, my shame became lighter but also exposed hundreds of wounds still bleeding. Each injury required a deeper look, which led to understanding and knowledge, which led to healing and restoration. With more and more healing, there came the need to learn a whole new way of thinking. The lies would need to be replaced with truth. With God, and through April, I rewrote my story. I gave God thirty days, and God gave me freedom from shame. Since He was right, I decided I would give Him thirty more days, maybe more.

CHAPTER 2

Origin Story

Born

In *To Kill a Mockingbird*, author Harper Lee writes, "...you can choose your friends but you sho' can't choose your family, an' they're still kin to you no matter whether you acknowledge 'em or not, and it makes you look right silly when you don't."[1] I am not foolish, so recognizing where I came from—my family of origin—was the first step when April asked me to complete the timeline of my life.

To understand where you are, you must know where you have been, where you come from. To make sense of who you are today, you have to consider and acknowledge your roots. I now know that what seemed utterly normal when I was growing up left me with a bad case of shame and a dangerous hunger for affirmation and affection.

I am not blaming my parents for the trauma of abuse I experienced or the life that happened after. They were doing the best they could to raise three children while enduring their own secrets. . Scripture reminds us over and over of our flawed nature. "For *all* have sinned and fall short of the glory of God" (Romans 3:23, NIV, emphasis mine). My grandparents were a product of their upbringing, however flawed. Then, my parents became a product of their upbringing by my grandparents. I am a product of how my parents raised me, and my children will bear the scars—and gifts—of the way I reared them.

To understand where I learned shame, where most of us learn shame, I had to look at where I was born.

My mother is the oldest of six siblings, and my father is the youngest of four sons. Birth placed me as the oldest of three siblings. Born in the early sixties, I am a child of the seventies. I was raised on *Star Trek* and *Gilligan's Island*, and witnessed the birth of Taco Bell, Wendy's, and Nacho Cheese Doritos.

When I attended elementary school, the girls wore knee-length dresses, knee-high socks, and black Mary Jane shoes. The boys had crew-cuts and tucked their shirts in their belted pants that stayed at their waist. Teachers wore heels and modest dresses with sweaters draped carefully across their shoulders. My first-grade teacher, Mrs. McDaniel, kept her sweater in place with a rhinestone brooch pinned to each side of her sweater's collar, a chain dangling in the space between. She spoke softly, calling us "children," and wrote with perfect precision between the solid and dotted lines on the green chalkboard. In Mrs. McDaniel's class, we learned to read words from books with pictures of Dick and Jane and their dog named Spot.

We lived in suburban Arkansas. At the time, our family was considered lower middle class, and by that I mean we had everything we needed but nothing extra. If there were money issues, my sister, brother, and I never knew. When we were teenagers, our high school experienced an influx of students from the affluent neighborhoods constructed nearby. That was when I began to understand that what we had was enough, but not much. Our clothes were not stylish but practical. We did not take summer vacations and drive a new car on our sixteenth birthdays. I compared myself to the popular girls all of my school days, and I always fell short.

In the summer, we stayed barefoot, outside, and out of sight until dusk when my father let out a high-pitched, ear-splitting whistle. He was able to make this whistle sound by putting his thumb and pointer finger on the sides of his mouth. That high-pitched sound was distinct, and everyone in the neighborhood knew what it meant. That whistle was his signature call, and his children understood that once you heard the call, you had minutes to appear at the table, cleaned and ready for dinner. Those who did not comply would draw attention to themselves and, depending on my mother's mood and my fathers' temper, could suffer the consequences.

My grandmother lived within spitting distance of our backyard, and I spent most of the hot, humid southern Arkansas summers at her house. Her tiny three-bedroom home was my sanctuary. I was welcome in the kitchen and always welcome to help myself to the Little Debbie snack cakes stacked on the counter. She would pour me a glass of the sweetest iced tea to wash down the oatmeal pies.

Mamaw, which I called her with emphasis on the "maw," made me feel noticed. I never felt as if she would hide the snacks and pour out the tea if I misbehaved or made too much noise. I could leave my fear on the other side of the creaky screen door to the porch. At Mamaw's, there was nothing wrong with me.

Being the first grandchild, I was my grandmother's first experience with children who were not her own. She raised six children, and, by all accounts, bent under the pressure. Who wouldn't? She was never married to my grandfather but claimed a common-law marriage, which was legal at the time in my grandfather's home state of Louisiana, but they lived in Arkansas. To add even more confusion, my grandfather was still married when he and my young grandmother started a life together. No denying the roots are tangled.

There is much I do not know about my grandmother's life. The details are murky, and my family admits she kept many secrets not even they know. Secrets on top of secrets piled on more secrets became

our family's legacy. Things never discussed in the light become a
way of life passed from one generation to the next—secret shame
inherited by the next generation.

One thing Mamaw did not keep secret
was Jesus. It is because of Mamaw that I
know Jesus.

*One thing
Mamaw did
not keep secret
was Jesus.*

Each Sunday, she would drag my
siblings and me to a small, red brick,
white-steepled church. We sat at the end of
a pew near the tall narrow windows. When
the church service began, the sunlight from

the outside streamed through the amber-colored glass and made my
skinny legs a funny orange color. Bible in her lap, her purse between
us, we listened to the hell, fire, and brimstone preaching. Without
fail, every Sunday the pastor we called Brother Ed would become so
passionate that he would pound the wooden pulpit with his fist, march
down the three stairs of the stage, tear off his suit coat, fling it across
the front pew, and begin pacing the aisles. "Repent," he would holler.

According to Brother Ed, I was going to hell, and hell sounded
like a place I did not want to go. He had no trouble convincing me
that I was a sinner. I knew there was something wrong with me. But it
was ultimately his description of the love of Jesus that enraptured me.

The love of Jesus.

The kind of love Jesus offered was not dependent on whether I
made good grades or cleaned my plate at dinner. His attention did
not depend on whether I was good enough or quiet enough. In fact,
according to the preacher, Jesus loved me no matter how bad I was—
and I knew there was something bad about me. For the first time,
I did not have to earn love and attention. He loved me just as I was.

When I was around nine years old, I stood next to my grandmother during the invitation at the end of the sermon just like I always

did. "I Surrender All," was playing on the ancient organ, and every voice in the sanctuary lifted up praise. My mind was swirling, telling me to go to the altar and to stay where I was. Go. Stay. I wanted so desperately to go—to know the love of Jesus. When I finally stopped listening to the voices in my head and took a step toward the preacher, I remember the world falling away. Maybe from nerves, maybe from God, but I couldn't see anything but the preacher standing near the altar. I wept and wept and wept, hardly able to answer his question, "Are you a sinner?"

"Yes," I said, "and I want to have Jesus." I wept some more, and Brother Ed handed me the hanky from his pocket.

There would be a forty or more year stretch between that moment and my next true encounter with Jesus. Of course, no one knows another's heart, and this lapse between the two meetings may leave some thinking that moment was not a true surrender to God. I disagree. As you will see through my story of shame, abuse, and living with the secret for most of my life, God never left me. Jesus was always there, protecting me, comforting me, guiding me, loving me, even if I only allowed Him to do so from afar. In my shame, I could not see it, but after He, God, led me to counseling instead of leaving me to suicide, I know He saved me when I was nine to seal me as His, mark me as His child, so He could rescue me again when I was forty-nine.

Raised

On the surface, my childhood was not terrible when compared to others. There was always hot food, warm, dry shelter, and clean clothes to wear. That is not terrible. My siblings and I respected our parents, said yes ma'am and no sir, and acted like the well-raised children we were. The neighbors would attest that all seemed well, and we were good kids.

I can count on one hand how many times I was allowed to invite my few friends for a sleepover. When it did happen, or friends came home with me after school, they would never suspect we were anything but a normal family. My mother cooked. After a hard day of construction work, my father sat in his recliner, smoking cigarettes one after the other. If there was ever anyone else in the house besides my family, it was deafeningly quiet. But I knew it was a silence that could and would shatter easily, like walking on glass. You learn to tiptoe.

My parents married young. My father, twenty at the time, did not finish high school and worked as an ambulance driver. Before that, he left home at fourteen because his alcoholic, abusive stepfather chased him with a shotgun. Hiding from stepfather's anger, he lived with neighbors, friends, and relatives, sleeping on couches and floors wherever he could lay his head. A couple of summers, he lived in Kansas City, where he played semi-professional baseball during the day and worked in the basement of the local hospital at night. *He* had a terrible childhood.

My father met my mother at church where my grandmother, Mamaw, taught the teen Sunday School class. My mother and father eloped. Seventeen at the time, my mother was not old enough to get married and had a family friend sign the marriage certificate. Just months after they sat in the same Sunday School class, they were married by a justice of the peace in a rural town on Highway 365. Twenty-three years later, they would be divorced.

The first day I noticed that something was wrong in my parents' marriage happened on the day of my parents' anniversary. The year is not clear, maybe their eighth or ninth year of marriage. It was summer, and we lived in a tiny house on the side of a steep hill. Monday through Friday, my father worked out of town building churches, but on Friday afternoon, he would roll up in the driveway in his pickup truck smelling like sawdust and sweat. On the Friday of their anniversary, there was a brand-new motorcycle tied to the truck bed.

The tension was palpable. The hair on the back of my neck still prickles when I think about that afternoon. Of course, I cannot remember the exact exchange of words, but I remember the fear, the run-and-hide kind of fear. I am sure my mother did not expect a motorcycle for an anniversary gift, and I am sure my father knew that. She probably screamed and yelled, and he might have hit her as I have learned did happen more than I saw. Then he left. It may have been only two days, but it was an eternity to a child. This Friday, after this brutal exchange, was when I saw my mother do what she would do many, many times and what I would learn to do later—withdraw. She withdrew from the world. We called it sulking when I was older. She would cut off the world, her children included. She would mechanically get us ready for school, feed us, and care for our home, but emotionally she was gone, leaving me, my brother, and sister to care for ourselves.

This pattern of rage then withdrawal continued until after I left home at eighteen. From the outside, all seemed well, but behind the curtain of a normal family were violent raging outbursts from my father, followed by weeks of my mother's withdrawal into silence. There were days my parents never said a word to each other. We three kids learned to maneuver carefully between the anger and silence.

As a child, I desperately wanted to fix it, to make my mother smile and calm my father's anger. My mother always told me that I was a perfect child. Never cried, never fussed, never anything. In my little mind, I believed that if I was good enough, quiet enough, smiled enough, my parents would be happy. It is a massive burden for a child to want to fix the world, and when I could not, I believed there must be something wrong with me.

Hunger

Most of us don't know what it feels like to go without food for more than a day, or even half a day. I imagine if I did go without something to eat that long, when I finally had food before me, I would eat everything in sight as if I may never eat again. Most people eat like that on Thanksgiving and Christmas and holidays where our favorite food is served only on those days. We eat until we have to slacken our belt or pants because we overate. We believe we will never ever have grandma's cornbread dressing or coconut pie or mom's yeast rolls again. We forget that we can have those things any time of the year. Stuffing, pie, and rolls are allowed and available any day of the year, but they taste better on the holidays.

But when someone is really hungry, even starved, they might do anything to be satisfied and stay that way.

When hungry for affirmation, affection, and love, some behave the same way as they do when turkey and dressing are offered at the Thanksgiving table. They lap up every ounce and morsel, because there is a fear that food will never be available again, at least not soon. Once someone learns how to get what they believe they hunger for, they work harder to taste just a bit of the sweet nectar again and again.

As I learned how to maneuver through the minefield of my parents' dysfunction, I learned that being somewhere near perfect meant getting noticed, which translated as love to me. So, I wanted to excel academically. And, in my teens, my circle of friends were the "good" kids from "good" families. In high school, I was a cheerleader and class president. Nothing was wrong with me on the outside. Tall, skinny, blonde, and, well, I might say, beautiful. (I'm laughing.) I tried hard to be as near perfection as I could.

Just under the surface, where no one could see, was a layer of shame.

However, just under the surface, where no one could see, was a layer of shame, shame that directed every thought about myself, every choice I made, every compromise I made on my value. I was hungry for attention, to be noticed.

At eleven, that hunger would lead to a moment that changed my life.

The street through our neighborhood made a circle. You entered and exited the area on the same road. Our house was positioned in the inner part of the circle. From our windows, you could see the neighbors on all sides, in front, beside, and behind. My mother always made it clear that we could not go into the neighbors' houses, ever. Some were allowed with special permission, and then only for an allotted amount of time, and, being the obedient child, I did not go into the neighbors' houses, ever. Well, unless it was the house of a young boy, who smiled at a little girl hungry for attention.

That summer day, my siblings and I were staying with my grandmother. Riding my pink bicycle around the circle street of our neighborhood, I was stopped at the mailbox by the teenage boy who lived in the house you could see from our kitchen window. Long hair, as was the seventies style, bell-bottom jeans, and a tight t-shirt—was he talking to me? Me? I could hardly believe my good fortune.

Yes, he was talking to me, and even more, he invited me into his house for a cold bottle of Coke. He was talking to me, and he was going to give me a Coke. I knew I must be dreaming. This was the first time I disobeyed my mother, but it would not be the last. But, as the enemy whispers to us so often, "Just this once won't hurt."

Most of the moments between me stepping into the dark house and stepping out are blurry. I remember the Coke in a glass bottle, cold in my hand. I remember him grabbing my hand and urging me down the hall. I recall resisting at first and then succumbing to his insistence. I remember watching from the ceiling. I remember the sound of the snap on my jeans and him holding my hands above my head. I closed my eyes.

I never cried. I never uttered a sound except to say, "I'm sorry." I was sorry I messed up the bed and spilled the Coke and stained the white bedspread. I'm sorry.

CHAPTER 3

Fallout

The Struggle

The fallout of abuse is a lifetime of struggling with fear and shame. As a child, I did not understand what was happening. My yet to be developed brain swirled with fear and inaudible self-talk. In confusion, I would feel the effects of shame again and again. My thoughts would take me to the worst outcome of every situation. Even as an adult, I did not connect the past with the present. I believed that if I would not think about what happened, that moment would have no effect on me.

I wanted to forget everything, but the fallout would not let me. I vowed to never think about it nor speak of it. That would be a deadly decision.

> *I wanted to forget everything, but the fallout would not let me.*

When I first started seeing April for counseling, she occasionally assigned books to read as "homework" between sessions, and I ate it up. I devoured book after book

about sexual trauma, books about people living with trauma, books about healing from trauma, and books about how trauma changes victims' minds and bodies. Every page I turned slid another piece of the puzzle into place. I was beginning to understand what happened and see the fallout.

Abuse trauma had altered my mind, body, and soul, leaving me— as it does to just about every abuse survivor—with a heavy coat of fear and shame.

One of my "homework" books was *The Body Keeps the Score: Brain, Mind, and Body in the Healing of Trauma* by Dr. Bessel Van Der Kolk. The book is a staple of trauma counselors, and it helped me understand the physiology of trauma and the physical fallout. Some memories and details of the incident may be blurry in my memory, but my body remembers precisely what happened. In his research, Dr. Kolk found that "...overwhelming experiences affect our innermost sensations and our relationship to our physical reality—the core of who we are."[1] Trauma changes our emotional—and physical—makeup. The way we think and learn, the way in which we experience the world, is altered.

Put this new knowledge together with counseling treatment and the Holy Spirit, and everything that was blurred came into crystal clear focus. The trauma of abuse changed my physiology and the way I viewed the world. Dr. Kolk's explanation of the effects continued, "...trauma is not just an event that took place sometime in the past; it is also the imprint left by that experience on mind, brain, and body."[2] Trauma leaves an imprint on a person's very being. This information transformed the way I thought. I went from thinking, *There is something wrong with me,* to understanding the profound difference that something wrong happened to me, and I survived.

My whole life began to make sense. I now saw that the fear, the shame, the years of self-hatred, self-destruction, broken relationships, addiction, and bad choices were connected to a moment in time. This newfound knowledge was not an excuse, but awareness—and awareness is curative. Sexual abuse trauma is a physical, emotional, and mental wound that never fully heals but it can be mended and pain diminished. And with God, it can be used for good.

Fear was the first thing I felt on the day I was abused—an overwhelming fear that I would die. Often, my mind runs away with the memory of that moment, and there is an anxious tingling in my chest, and I take a deep breath. After a few seconds of self-talk and reminding myself that I am now an adult, I can go on. The "fear fallout" remains real, and it manifests at the most inopportune times.

One of those times happened a few years ago, when my husband, youngest son, and I spent a few days in St. Louis. At the last minute, we decided to take a leisurely drive north through the mountains of north Arkansas and spend a few summer days taking in the sights and watching a ballgame. I was able to reserve us a hotel room across from Busch Stadium, where we saw the Cardinals play the Pirates while the rain poured. And like every other tourist, we visited the towering iconic Gateway Arch, the symbol of St. Louis.

Lounging in the park at the base of the Arch, which is positioned on the banks of the Mississippi River and faces both east and west, my son and I sat, deciding whether we wanted to ride to the top. We lingered in the gift shop and wandered through the mini-museum as we watched people gather one by one to form the Disney-ride-like line to board the pod elevators that would take visitors 630 feet in the air. At the top, brave visitors can look out a tiny window and admire the landscape stretching east and west. After much discussion about whether we wanted to wait three hours to take a forty-five-minute elevator ride to spend five minutes looking out a window to take another forty-five-minute elevator ride to the ground, we agreed it might be a once-in-a-lifetime opportunity. We took our place in the snaking line.

The line to board the elevators wound down into the sub-basement level of the Arch. Nearly two hours later, it was our turn to be seated inside the pods. Inside the elevator pods were eight seats with no headroom. An adult could not stand fully upright.

To be clear, there were signs and warnings along the route toward the elevators that alerted the riders that this was coming. In red letters, on signs every twenty feet, warnings came. "If you experience anxiety in small places...," which translates to "Turn back now—before it's too late."

My inner coach denied the warnings and the increased heart rate. *You can do this. It's a once-in-a-lifetime chance. Your son is watching you.* I was committed, and I wanted to make memories with my son. As we approached the pods, I noticed my heart rate increase even more. If anyone looked closely, they could probably have seen my heart beating through my sweat-soaked t-shirt. Our turn came to be seated, and I could feel sweat running down my back, although we were deep in an air-conditioned cave. With weak knees, I sat next to my son beside the door. But just seconds before the doors were closed, I shot an arm out the door to keep it from closing,

"This is not going to happen," I shouted at the surprised attendant who was ushering people to fill the pod.

I grabbed my son's arm, and we exited the car before the doors closed. Embarrassed and beginning to feel faint, I followed the signs out of the basement and into the sun and oxygen. I could breathe again.

We laugh about it now, and my son tells stories about how mom panicked in a pod. It does sound like a panic attack or a sudden attack of claustrophobia. It was both. Now, filled to the brim with knowledge and understanding, I see this reaction to the possibility of being in a small, confined space without the ability to exit when I wanted, stemmed from a moment way back in my childhood. Forty years back.

Fight, Flight or Freeze

In my reading, I learned that when people are confronted with a traumatic event, like sexual abuse, our bodies have been designed by a thoughtful Creator to react without intervention. The millisecond a threat is imminent, our bodies are flooded with hormones like adrenaline, cortisol, and norepinephrine. This hormone soup makes you ready to fight or run from danger. When the threat is over, the hormones go back to normal, and you will probably need a nap to recover from the hormone high.

There is a third response—to freeze. When neither fight nor flight is possible, and you are faced with potential harm or death, our bodies "play dead." When freezing is the only way to survive, our bodies release pain-killing endorphins and opioids. Our bodies relax and breathing slows. If we survive, the "fear chemicals" dissolve, and the body will often tremble uncontrollably.

With traumatized children, as was my experience, that feeling of fear never ends. The fear is forever, and each time that memory is triggered, the response is the same, even throughout adulthood. Fear becomes a constant companion. I would always be on high alert waiting and watching for another threat. And the perceived *Fear becomes a constant companion.*

threat was triggered when I tried to board a small elevator pod in St. Louis. The trauma is never "one and done," especially if it is a secret trauma that only the victim and the perpetrator know.

Forty years later, I felt that fear. Sitting in my car, waiting for my son to exit the high school, scrolling through my social media feed, I was afraid of the face in my social media feed.

The reality is that a ten-minute encounter continued to impact my life for over forty years. A second reality is that it always will.

I will always be gripped with the irrational fear of being in tight places. Crowded elevators will ever leave me woozy because the fear response I learned four decades ago will set off the same alarms when the doors are about to close.

Being held down without the hope of escape and with the fear of harm is seared into my memory. But once the immediate danger passed, the real enemy emerged. Shame manifested in my actions and choices as a people-pleasing, perfection-seeking, overachieving child, seeking any affirmation and attention. This unanswered need would lead to more fear and shame and pain. Secrets, shame and fear painted a target.

Target

As a scared little girl, I always felt I did not belong anywhere. I felt ugly, awkward, and did not fit. I was an outsider, even in my family. So, I stuck to the shadowy places and quietly waited for someone to notice me. This is a symptom of shame, I later discovered. Children cannot develop a sense of worth under the weight of shame, especially when they carry shame that is not theirs. And often, this puts a target on their backs.

Today, there are a myriad of public service announcements about abuse awareness. One shows celebrities touting "It's On Us" to intervene and stop the violence. Another admonishes viewers to say something if they suspect abuse, inferring they should watch for signs.

Only in recent years have abuse, trauma, and shame become topics discussed openly. Sharing your shame story or addressing fear and sexual abuse were taboo decades ago, and there continues to be generations that stay silent. They do not understand that shame begets shame. If we are encouraged to keep secrets and not talk about what happened, we feel even more ashamed to tell our story.

The only way to stop the harmful effects of shame and abuse is to bring it into the light.

Shame cannot breathe in the light. But when it is hidden deep, covered, and dismissed, it grows into a monster devouring little girls and grown women. That is the reason I crusade for women to have a safe, compassionate place to tell their stories. Telling shines light on the darkness.

Forty years ago, I believed some people could sense that I held a secret. Some, I think, ignored the signs, and others looked away, too busy or indifferent. There are no distinct memories, but there is no way an eleven-year-old child who was violently sexually abused did not display signs. Bouts of uncontrollable tears, becoming withdrawn, avoiding school and friends—there must have been a sign.

There was a teacher I remember from high school who I believe sensed a problem. She was kind, compassionate, encouraging, never pushing me. She looked at me and not over me. Still, others took advantage of the silence and perpetrated more abuse.

There is evidence that predators possess a kind of sixth sense where they can pick out the shameful, the compliant, the secret keepers. Couple that with an accepted silence and denial that abuse exists, and you set up a predator to openly prowl. They are everywhere.

Once a Sunday School teacher, a man, singled me out from the other kids, in a room alone at church, and asked me, "What's under that shirt?" I remember the moment because I believe tidbits of our history become indelible spots on our memories from the connected overwhelming emotion. Emotions are tied to our most vivid memories, and the feeling I felt that day was fear, the kind that makes you freeze in your tracks like I did just a year or two before. I'm sure the Sunday School teacher could smell my fear.

Thankfully, by God's protection, nothing happened. Perhaps the Sunday School teacher was testing to see if I would comply and keep quiet. Either his opportunity passed, or my response was not sufficient proof I would comply. Either way, only by God's grace was I protected.

Most of the time, predators don't give up so easily. Sometimes the shame and fear entice the predator beyond his ability to resist, like sharks when there is blood in the water.

In the small town where I grew up, I went to a small school a ten-minute bus ride down the highway. Everyone on our street rode the same bus that stopped to let kids off at the elementary and high school. In junior high, now about fourteen, I got on and off the bus like everyone else every school day—until I didn't.

The bus driver knew my name and my father's name and mother's name, too. He knew my sister and brother and even my grandmother. He was a familiar face to us all. And watching me day after day, I am positive he could see the fear and shame.

When I was in the eighth grade, he began to take a particular interest in me. It was innocent at first. "Smile," he would say as I stepped down off the bus at the end of our driveway. My immature, naive little girl self could not discern his intent. I only knew that he saw me, and I needed to be seen.

After a while, he would say, "Wait, I want to talk to you a minute." I would step between the first two seats on the bus as my sister and brother and all the other neighborhood kids departed the bus and disappeared. Parents were not waiting for us. Most of the parents on our street worked and would not be home for another two hours. We were all latchkey kids. No one would miss us if we were late, and he knew that.

The talks turned into touching, which led to sitting in his lap. "We can't tell anyone, because this is our special friendship. People wouldn't understand."

Frozen with fear of him and of what my parents might say or do, I was silent again. Compliant. Secrets building. Shame growing. Fear freezing my senses. The after-school attention went on for a semester. I was so happy when Christmas break came, but I feared its end.

We are all asking the same question. Where is God? Why would a good, loving God allow a little girl to endure abuse—again? Why would He allow her to know this kind of pain in her heart and soul? We will never be able to answer that question this side of heaven, and I must accept that truth. I also hang onto the truth that God did not design a world where one in six girls and one in eight boys will be abused before they turn eighteen. No, it is evil that creates these facts. It is evil in the world that ruins young lives and destroys little hearts. Let's face it—evil is in the world, and, in my case, it drove the school bus and lived around the corner.

I may not understand why these things happened, but this I do know: God sees every day of our lives, and the repeated attempts and successes of evil on a little girl are not a surprise to Him. He was there. I could not have known it then, but I see it now through the lens of a grown-up, Jesus-following woman. God protected me. He protected my mind and body because He made me able to endure and persevere.

To protect my mind, I was able to dissociate, live outside myself, and separate myself from the evil. Fear hormones kicked into hyper-drive, numbing me to any pain to protect my body. And here's the excellent part. God knew I would experience an emotional break-down driving down the highway four decades later, and He would say, "See a counselor." He prepared the healing in advance, placing a counselor made just for me in my path. He protected me time after time. He watched over me through self-hatred, self-destruction, addiction, and more than one attempt to end my life.

He protected me for such a time as this. To tell the secret, finally. To bring it into the light. To find healing. To write it down, at last.

He knew I would be sitting at this computer today, on a beautiful summer Sunday morning, writing. Telling. He saw me.

At the moment, during the fear, I was not thinking about God while I sat on this man's lap more than once a week. No, I was surviving and coping the best way a little girl could. God did not abandon me. I could not see it then, and as I said before, it would be years later before I could see clearly that God was there. Often, that is how we see God's steadfast love and faithfulness—in the rearview mirror.

When these memories flash across my mind, especially while I am writing them to the world, I must replace them with the truth. I know the aftershocks of abuse will rise and fall until I am called heavenward and home. I must fend off the darkness and change the scene. I have to imagine that during those horrific watershed moments that changed the trajectory of my life, Jesus held my face in His hands and whispered, "You are not alone. I see you, and I love you." Four decades ago, I could not have pictured Jesus holding me, seeing me, and loving me, and I continue to struggle with believing it now, but that does not make it any less true.

It is also my belief that God rescued and protected me. There should be no doubt the bus stop moments in my life were significantly discussed during counseling. As April and I pulled back the onion layers that were my childhood, we spent several sessions dissecting this chapter on my timeline. For so many years, I carried the responsibility for what the bus driver did. It was my fault he did what he did. I even convinced myself that it was harmless, that my memory of the days was blurred and it must not have happened. These guilty thoughts are normal in abuse. The victim becomes the perpetrator or minimizes the event. But April helped me remember a tidbit I forgot, and it changed my view of the events. My little girl self ended the bus driver's advances. Some kind of inner strength that can only be credited to a protective God rose up and showed me how to escape. After Christmas break, I simply went from being the last off the bus to the first. That is a little girl who will survive.

CHAPTER 4

Running Away

New York, New York

The genes I inherited from my mother's side of the family made me long, lean, and tall in my teens. My mother's brothers are all well over six feet tall, and her sister is also over six feet tall. Today, I claim my father's genetic make-up, shorter, rounder, and plump. When I was younger, though, in my teens, every coach of every girls' high school sport recruited me because of my height. Hungry for attention and affirmation, I tried them all.

I failed miserably at basketball. I could not do two things at one time—dribble and run. In junior high, I jumped on the cheerleading bandwagon. My height and build made me ideal for the girl who supported the wobbly human pyramids. Neither of these sports satisfied me, and my performance was mediocre.

What I could do was run. Long legs and long strides were a benefit. And I loved it. By high school, I was staying after school to practice with the girls' track team, and the coach assigned me the 110-yard hurdle event. Probably because no one else wanted to try.

Yes, hurdles. Not only would I be running, but I would have to maintain precise timing and cadence to clear each of ten hurdles.

33

If I were off just one second, my knees and shins would suffer as they often did. Despite all of the practice and the pain, and an occasional case of road rash, there was no better thrill than crossing the finish line.

And running became a way of life.

After high school, I left home pretty much within weeks. I was ready to be free from my mother's judging eye and my father's anger. I ran away, first to an apartment with two other girls, which ended badly, then to New York City.

I was eighteen, one suitcase and twenty-five dollars in my pocket. I manipulated the purchase of the flight by writing a check my bank account could not cover. I told my mother I would be back in three weeks. I lied. I had a one-way ticket.

Waiting for me in New York City was a man I met just weeks before. We met in the mall where we both worked. I worked in the large department store on one end of the mall, and he worked in the small liquor store on the opposite end. I stopped in one day and bought a Diet Coke from the refrigerator section, near the counter he stood behind. We talked and laughed, and soon we began dating. I believed in love at first sight. He was ten years older and would move to the City before me to attend art school.

I believed he was the answer, my savior. He would, with his unconventional attitude and artist charm, be the one who would lift me above my shame, or so I believed. He would make me right again. With the scene of the crime two thousand miles behind me, I believed he would cure the dull pain radiating from my core. I would be wrong. No human can heal that kind of brokenness.

At first, we lived on a honeymoon-like bliss. There was certainly no money to live any other way. Before I arrived, my boyfriend scouted the city for an apartment where we would live together. He found a one-bedroom, fixer-upper, on the sixth floor of a six-story

pre-World War II building in the middle of Spanish Harlem in upper
Manhattan. It was dirt cheap. Probably because the kitchen barely
had a floor. It did, however, have a lovely view of the Bronx just over
the Harlem River.

Between the two of us, we owned
less than nothing. For a bed, we rode the
subway from the upper tip of Manhattan
to Chinatown in Lower Manhattan to
purchase a full-sized, six-inch thick piece
of foam. We carried it on the train back
the same way we came, laid it on the floor,
covered it with a sheet, and called it a bed.
That was the first piece of "furniture" in

*The problem
with running
away is that you
either have to
keep running or
go home.*

our apartment. After our first month in Harlem, we managed to
find milk crates and chairs in the trash on the sidewalk to complete
the ensemble.

The problem with running away is that you either have to keep
running or go home.

Two years into playing house, the honeymoon ended. The Big
Apple lost its glamour, and I realized the dull ache of shame had
returned. At first, I was too busy being a tourist in New York to
notice. Then, months turned into a year and then two years, and the
doldrum of making ends meet turned into dissatisfaction. The pain
returned, this time bigger than ever.

Though I tried to convince myself that living with a man without
being married was modern and what people were doing those days, my
heart knew the truth. Shame begets shame. I saw myself as shameful
and unworthy of the best in a relationship, so I settled. I was not
worthy of a commitment, honor, and adoration. I would settle for
crumbs. And crumbs were what I received, heaping shame on shame
and confirming everything I believed about myself.

So, it was time to run, and I did. I spent the next two years and change living alone in a tiny studio apartment in the low rent district of the Upper East Side of Manhattan. To some, this sounds fascinating, like something out of a sitcom on television—single girl in the big city. That was not the reality.

Barely able to pay the rent, I depended on the gifts of men. One winter, I needed a coat, and one came wrapped with a bow. The only thing I had to do was, well, you can fill in the blanks. No money to buy food, the same. The shame was growing too enormous to bear. To kill the aching that increased with each "gift," I learned the numbing effects of alcohol, various drugs, and cocaine. It was the eighties.

I knew I was in the middle of raging sin, putting myself in countless dangerous situations, yet, other than losing my job, I believe God protected me from harm. Again, I should have been dead. But I wasn't. What did God want with me? What good could I be to a holy God? What use did He have for a piece of trash?

Thinking back on those days, I see divine intervention all over my days and nights. I was self-destructing, and I loved it. Abuse strips you of control over your world. Living dangerously and putting myself in dire situations made me feel, falsely, in control. Putting myself in risky places with even more dangerous people and engaging in blatant sin became the way to kill the ache and prove I was as unworthy of love as I suspected. It was anger wrapped in a coat of self-loathing. It was like saying, "See, I told you I was damaged and worthless. See how I act? There's nothing God or anyone can do to fix me."

There were many instances to illustrate my self-destructive behavior and the saving protection of God, but a single instance stands out in my memory. There was one night where I could have easily been assaulted or worse. Why I remember this particular incident is unclear. Maybe it was especially frightening. We tend to remember events associated with great emotion. Perhaps I remember this individual night of destruction because God wants to remind me that

He protected me. He fought for me, even when I strayed and was lost. He rescued me.

It must have been a weekend night, because I was under the influence, and, somehow in my state of mind, I found myself in a crowded, smoky, loud bar in a dangerous part of the city. Those I came with abandoned me. Inebriated, not knowing where I was and surrounded by people in a similar state who could have taken advantage, I somehow woke up in my apartment on the opposite side of town. Unharmed physically. Undamaged except for the ton of regret and shame added to the already heavy load.

The sin and numbing escalated until I lost my job. It was the first time I was fired. Saying I was humiliated does not describe the depths of shame at that point. No job. No, well, nothing. Determined not to go home, I considered my options. New job? No, that bridge was still smoldering. Friends? No, if they could fire me, too, they had already. What was I good at? What was my talent? In my fear and desperation, prostitution was looking good. I was already on that train. Gratefully, I had no idea how to turn it into a living.

I could not run any farther. I had to go home.

Two weeks later, I boarded a plane using a ticket my mother paid for. Everything I owned was once again in my suitcase, and I had no money in my pocket. The prodigal daughter was going home.

Prodigal

"Prodigal" means to be wasteful or squander resources. The word describes one who throws away what he or she possesses in resources, whether it is money, reputation, or grace. To me, "prodigal" does not accurately describe me at the time. You have to have assets to waste them. I owned nothing but my clothes. I ran away from home with nothing and came home with less than nothing. There was nothing to squander, not even a reputation.

The better description might be the return of "the lost daughter," "the broken daughter," "the empty daughter." That twenty-something girl was unrecognizable. My body and soul were sick. I was bone thin, shoulders slumped, head down, and my eyes sported dark circles. A good physical examination would have determined I was anemic and undernourished. I was a ghost.

By the time I returned to my childhood' home, only my father lived in the house. My mother and father divorced some time while I was in New York, and my mother moved to an apartment in town. After more than twenty years of rage and emotional dysfunction, something had to break. It is no comfort, but I saw the end coming from a long way off. Their divorce was imminent.

For my return, no one met me on the road when they saw me coming. Nor was there a feast or fattened calf. There was no fanfare, confetti, or fireworks. There were heavy sighs, and everyone avoided direct eye contact, and the feel of disappointment was so heavy you could hold it in your hand. There were no questions. Perhaps, no one wanted to know what happened. Probably, if they asked, they did not want to know the answer.

Strangely, I was glad they could not bring themselves to ask. I would have lied anyway to avoid adding more weight to my cloak of shame. I feared their summation of the past five years. "See, I told you it would be a disaster, that you would fail. You embarrassed us and brought shame with your foolishness. See, I told you so." They would be correct.

As I have said before, my father and family were not intentionally adding to my shame. They were not aware of what happened in the house behind ours forty years before. They acted out of a perfectly human response. That's what we do, avoid the uncomfortable. But their silence, their avoidance, their lack of celebration—in my little girl existence, that translated to being not good enough for notice.

Of course, I dreamed of the return being more celebratory. I wanted the unspoken disappointment to instead be joy. I wanted my family to say, "We are so glad you have returned. Here's a new coat, and a new monogrammed ring for your hand. Sit, you must be exhausted, and let us celebrate your return." Cue the barbeque. But it did not happen.

Instead, I was worse than when I left, my secret now buried beneath layers and layers of shame. I lived in a prison I had built and believed I deserved. Maybe I could try harder to be better.

That's the key. Try harder. Be better.

I thought if I just tried harder, then everything would be right again. If I did something remarkable, my family, those in my life, would look at me differently. *I'll try harder, put more effort into being good and perfect, and then they will see what a good girl I am. I will have value. I will be worthy of a celebration.* I was an eleven-year-old little girl begging for affirmation again, pleading for attention and affection.

Look at me, Daddy. I'll be good. I can do better.

I tried harder to be better.

Mask

Well-known shame researcher and speaker, Brené Brown defines shame this way, "Shame is the intensely painful feeling or experience of believing we are flawed and therefore unworthy of acceptance and belonging."[7] Shame is universal. No one escapes. And we expend enormous amounts of energy to cover it and control it.

When running away only made the shame deepen, I convinced myself that if no one could see it, then it did not exist. I tried to cover my secret and shame.

Trying to cover shame is exhausting because it is not just an emotion. It is a force. It controls every thought, action, decision, choice, and relationship. How you perceive your value is directly affected by your level of shame. Shame fuels the fight to be better because you believe something is wrong with you and therefore have little or no value. The shame becomes a fire in your belly that you try to extinguish.

Trying to improve our outside, we believe, will fix the inside and cool the burning pain. Shame says, *If I can just be a better wife, a better mother, a better co-worker, a better cook, a better driver, a better* _____ *(fill in the blank). If I could just be better somehow, no one will know the worst of me.*

Shame strips away our ability to see clearly. It magnifies flaws, creates insecurities, and augments inabilities. Debilitating shame becomes your identity, and being better becomes the mask worn to hide who you believe you are because that is the greatest danger—being found out.

Within a few weeks of returning home, my body recuperated, and I was ready to find something or someone to fix me. I was on the hunt for some way to show that I could be better than what I was. I could, at last, put the secret away and forget.

Without being fully aware of what I was doing, I remade myself into the opposite of the big city girl. I wanted my family, and then the world, to see me in a new light, to see me the way I believed they wanted to see me. Shame does that. To cover the shame and secrets, I became a chameleon, changing my appearance to match the environment. I turned into the girl that whoever I hung my security on expected. My personality, the way I dressed, even the food I ate mirrored my surroundings and what was expected.

I put on a mask, and everything else about me became the costume. My plan worked until a tear in the costume threatened to expose the actor underneath and pull back the curtain to expose me and my secret shame. Every time, I molded and bent myself into others' expectations, I failed. Sometimes, I tired of the game. Other times, I believe the people around me got a peek at the brokenness and left the game. Wearing a mask to cover who I thought I was became a futile exercise in hide-and-seek.

Being someone I was not required all of my energy. The masks went on and off like fireflies on a summer night. One person required me to be a smoking drinking party girl. Another expected a prim, pulled together Sunday School good girl. Yet another wanted someone to be a servant and caregiver.

This all came from the day the neighbor boy took what was not his and then pushed me out the door before his parents came home. That little girl, still shaky after the pain of the physical act, was abandoned by the person who, for the first time, exhibited interest and genuine concern. Twisted as it was, my little girl self could not separate the good from the bad. It was impossible. To "her," it was pain and tenderness, wrong and right, love and abandonment. It was "our" secret, both special and taboo.

My little girl will forever be connected to those moments. Even now, it is not something that a surgeon or even my wonderful earthly counselor can separate from who I am.

When I was raped, every part of my being ached for attention, both physical and emotional. I disobeyed my parents to be in that boy's house. As a little girl, I would do whatever I needed to find love and affirmation. I would be whatever you needed.

And no matter how little sense it makes, when he took my innocence, he left an imprint of how to feel wanted and maybe loved. The enemy twisted precious love out of shape and turned it into an act of power and evil that left a dark hole. For four decades, I would try to find something to fill that hole once and for all. No matter how I turned myself inside out, the hole only grew.

Putting on a mask and becoming whoever I needed to be to survive became a way of life, so easy to do that I didn't know I was doing it. Sometimes it worked. Other times it did not.

CHAPTER 5

Survivor

The Game

In a shame-filled, abuse-broken heart, survival is the name of the game. Coping with the pain and fear is a matter of life or death. Imagine you were diagnosed with a fatal illness. The doctors and medical experts determine the only way to survive is to figure it out yourself. And you can never tell another person you are sick. Not your husband. Not your mother. Not your dearest, most trusted friend. Not one person. If you do, you will die.

What? You scream, "I have never had this disease before, and I have no earthly idea how to heal myself. How can I treat myself? And I can't tell anyone?"

"It's a secret," they say. "You might die if you tell, or it could cause more harm than cure."

That's what surviving looked like for me and a multitude of abuse survivors. The quiet game.

The definition of a survivor is a person who continues to function or prosper despite opposition, hardship, or setbacks.[1] The dictionary says it is a person who copes well with difficulties in their life. That's why I always have trouble labeling myself as a "survivor." The hat doesn't seem to fit my head. I could function, but not prosper. Hardships and setbacks only changed the way I coped, and I did not cope well with difficulties. If I wasn't creating them, I was trying to endure them.

Surviving, for me, changed according to my situation. During my time in New York, it meant not starving, keeping the electricity on, not being alone, numbing the pain, and keeping the secret.

Surviving in the city depended more on me than on the help of family and friends. I was anonymous and could morph into anyone I needed to be to survive. We already know that an abuse-scarred mind is a people-pleaser, doing whatever is necessary to make everyone happy. For my survival in New York—to make people happy and willing to help me—I assumed the role of a "party girl."

I was a classic textbook "party girl." Still a teenager when I arrived, I was confused and unaware that shame and fear led my every thought and choice. I am sure I was in hyper-survival mode. The faux friends I claimed in those days wanted someone who wanted to have fun. And, so, I became the life of the party. I was flirty and willing to please. I was easy-going and always enjoyed a good time, and it did not matter what it took to have a good time. I would do it all if you promised to love me—drink, dance, run naked down the street—but if you showed any hint of possible pain, I could hate you in a heartbeat. I could loathe you more than myself, and that was hard to do. I would drop you like an empty beer can.

My survival depended on avoiding hurt and abuse. The self-protection probably did not happen all at once. My mind and heart were always sniffing out possible sources of pain. A little tidbit of trust crushed or a morsel of commitment denied, and, like the masks I wore, the protective shields ascended. My party girl persona was my protector. It worked for a while, but it did not remove the problem. The party girl persona could not erase a deep secret and a ton of shame.

Shame convinced me that if I could just fix myself, be who I needed to be to survive, life would be grand, and all my problems would be solved. So many days, I dreamed of being someone new, someone who could be loved and wanted. If I could only fix myself.

If only I were good enough, everyone would love me.

If I were prettier or smarter or more fun, I would be seen.

If only I could forget, then I would not know shame.

The "party girl" was one attempt to fix myself. Later, I swapped that persona out for the "good girl." From an abuse-healing perspective, I see how it was all a matter of self-protection and survival, this flip-flopping between personalities. By becoming who others wanted me to be, I trusted that I would not be harmed again, that I would feel loved and wanted.

When I left New York and came home, I left the party girl on the tarmac at LaGuardia Airport. However, I did keep her shame, which had grown to the height of a mountain. I needed a new fix. Swing the pendulum, and I became a "good girl."

Without being fully aware, I went from the party girl from New York to the good girl from Arkansas—a 360-degree turn.

The party girl and good girl were not just outward manifestations of my inward struggle to wrestle my secret and shame into submission. These sisters—secret and shame—helped me relate, although in an emotionally unhealthy way, with people. Even into my twenties and thirties, all right, and forties, I needed validation and affirmation that I was loveable. If I had to reshape my identity to get that, I would and often did.

My party girl and good girl personas were born out of abuse. Using their strengths and weaknesses, I maneuvered through the world. Without these protective personas, the abuse, the depression, the self-loathing and shame would have eaten me alive. I would not have survived. Without my facades, I would have been a raging animal. My mind was turbulent with fear, always ready to run or fight. These personalities kept my fear calm, my thoughts and energy spent on being a good girl or a good time girl. They stayed between me and the reality of my pain and anger.

We all have our ways of relating to others and the world. So many factors mold our relational style. They range from where you are born, your education, your income to the sins committed against you, and the sins you commit. But the common factors we all have are our need to be loved, our fear of being alone, our contempt for being used, and our need to control our world.[3] God didn't make us to worry about being unloved, alone, abused, or controlled, but when Eve took the first bite, she ushered in loneliness, feeling unloved, being used by others, and needing to control everything about our lives. I can't help but wonder, if the abuse did not happen, would I still have waffled between one persona and another? Would there have been a party girl or a good girl? How would my life have been different?

The shame I found as a little girl and the shame I heaped on through my teens, added to the shame I carried home from New York, became unbearable. There was no place, no relationship, no person where I could lay it down. I was a prisoner in my own body and mind, which would take over when I felt scared. I felt crazy. I wanted someone, anyone to fix me.

Fixer-Upper

We know that quick fixes never last. Slapping a band-aid on a bleeding wound or a piece of duct tape on a broken arm will not heal the problem. The do-it-yourself repair would quickly disintegrate, leaving a much bigger issue. I am the DIY person at our house. I try to make minor repairs, such as patching holes in the wall and changing our showerheads. Sometimes they work, and sometimes I just need to call a professional—or my brother-in-law. So, you can imagine the damage done when I applied quick fixes to my survival.

I tried to fix myself many times. It would start out like those HGTV shows where the super talented fixers buy a dilapidated ugly house. In about ninety TV minutes, the house is transformed. New floors, new furniture, new curtains, and the place is spectacular. So much so that you might buy a ticket to tour the place. And they make it look so easy. It's not.

My quick fixes included putting on masks to cover the scars and painting personalities to hide the inner wreckage. I tucked the secret and shame safely away to forget it and prayed it would never get loose. No fix lasted. Not one do-it-yourself repair job stayed fixed. I was a constant fixer-upper, forever twisting and changing myself, mending and repairing where I saw weak places and cracks. It was the only way to survive and not give in to the burden of shame.

My first husband unknowingly was the next quick fix to my fixer-upper.

I was wearing the mask of a fun-loving, emotionally-stable, self-sustaining woman when I met my him—in a bar. Not the ideal situation, I know. That should have been the first red flag, but red flags and warnings were silent on my radar. I dismissed them regularly.

He was charming, aloof, and ruggedly handsome. Wearing a buttoned-down shirt and faded jeans, smoking a cigarette and holding a beer in the other hand, I remember thinking he reminded me of the man in the Marlboro cigarette advertisements. The Marlboro Man. Around us, the music was loud, and the liquor was flowing. I passed him my phone number on a napkin. He did not call for three days. When he did, he invited me to a "lunch date." Sparks immediately fired and on went a new mask.

When we met, I was in survival mode again and looking for someone to help me. I wanted to be fixed, and I believed leaving my party girl high heels and low-cut blouses behind and exchanging them for a good girl gingham dress, apron, and sensible shoes would save me.

He married me under pretense. I didn't hold a gun to his head or blackmail him into saying, "I do," but looking at the scene from a distance of twenty-plus years, I see I was looking for a quick fix. My twisted, shame-filled imagination believed that he could erase the brokenness. He was disciplined, systematic, predictable, and stable. Just what a girl who was the opposite of all those things needed. His personality was the band-aid to my broken bleeding heart. It's not his fault that he couldn't fix me. He was not the right "duct tape." I needed something more miraculous.

My first husband is a good man, and I am profoundly regretful and remorseful for pretending to be someone I was not when he met me. Although we both have responsibility for how our marriage ended, I shoulder most of the blame. With all the chameleon-morphing, mask-making coping mechanisms in my toolbox of survival, he could never see the real me. I didn't even know the real me at that point in my life. My only objectives were hiding the secret and surviving. All I can say is, "Bless his heart."

It was apparent at the start that we were all mixed up. It was a kind of "shotgun wedding." We were dating about six months before the plus sign appeared on the pregnancy test stick. We were going to have a baby. Fire up the shock, fear, and anxiety. We said what most unmarried couples would say at that moment. "We have to get married."

His reverently Catholic mother and former Baptist father were disappointed but supportive. My mother was unmoved and my father unaware. So, we started planning the wedding. It would be a May wedding eight weeks in the future. I was so excited, and I convinced myself everything was going to be good, and I was good. Finally, I was worthy of love.

Between choosing wedding colors and ordering the napkins, I saw my new obstetrician who reported everything was well. He confirmed we were expecting and could hear the tiny heartbeat. Our baby would arrive sometime in the fall.

The wedding plans were progressing. We were living together then, and I remember thinking life was perfect. *I'm going to have a baby. I'm not alone, so I must be good enough to love.*

Just days before the happy day, the unimaginable happened. I miscarried the sweet child I would never know.

The doctor explained these things happen. Your body knows when there is a problem. All I heard was, "You are a failure at this, too. This is what you get for all you've done. It's your fault."

With devastation in my heart and fear moving in like a bulldozer, the wedding was still a go. If we were sitting at an intersection in a car, there would be caution lights blinking. But I ignored the signals. I believed getting married would fix me.

The ceremony and celebration were mixed with both beauty and trepidation. It was not my dream wedding, but lovely all the same. I set my expectations too high and before the "I do," I was disappointed, and my dream of love and being loved was already disintegrating.

I was so nervous that when the justice of the peace said to put the ring on my new husband's hand, I put it on the right hand and not the left. I don't think the guests noticed, nor did they know there was no baby.

My husband and I would have a second chance. Our first son was born a year later, and I remember it clearly. For a day, everything that haunted me was silent. For an hour, the only voice in my head was this perfect pink boy crying, bellowing out his very first sounds in this world. For one minute, all I knew was joy.

It was a Friday. The sun was shining. When the nurse placed him in my arms, I forgot where I was, who I was, and every day before that moment. There was no past, and I was not thinking about the future. There was only this tiny human who I wholly and instantly fell in love with. That baby was the light in my darkness. When I looked at his tiny red face, I felt, for the first time ever, unfathomable love.

I would feel that way again when our second son was born about three years later. For another day, I felt safe and saved, enveloped in an impenetrable bubble. It did not matter what was done to me or what I had done. I did not have to be a good or good time girl. There was only one thing—him.

These two precious boys consumed me. Now I knew life was perfect. This fixer-upper felt fixed.

Sabotage

The first few years of our marriage and the beauty of loving my children did temporarily fix me, but it was not happily ever after. The duct tape and Gorilla Glue would not hold my heart together. I was too broken.

We bought a little home and played house. My dream of being Donna Reed was upon me. I cooked, cleaned, and raised two boys with as much care as I knew, sans the apron and string of pearls Donna wore in *The Donna Reed Show*. There was a dog in the backyard and two cars in the driveway. The scene was picture perfect. We were living my dream. Until we weren't.

I can't even remember what triggered the survival mindset and sabotage that led to our divorce. It could have been a disagreement and harsh words and an angry tone of voice from my husband that unlocked my little girl's fear, shame, and pain. It was flight, fight, or freeze and I wanted to get away—to run.

On the inside—in my head—I became the same small girl who hid from my father's rage, who longed for affirmation and affection from my mother, and who knew deep shame from repeated sexual abuse. The outside may have grown up, but the inside of me, my heart and head, were still a scared little girl desperately wanting to be wanted.

Whatever sent me reeling back unleashed an assault on my emotional and mental state. I would be in survival mode again because I would interpret my husband's momentary unhappiness as unending. He didn't love me after all, I told myself. The volume of the voices in my head blasted and the lies played on repeat.

He can't love me because I am unlovable.

He is going to abandon me. I'll be alone and unable to take care of my children.

He doesn't want me anymore.

There is no way God loves you.

Survival is the name of the game, and sabotage is self-protection.

Out of respect for my children, my ex-husband, both of our families, and all who know me and my past, I'll not describe how my flight-fear response played out. Let's just say the shame sack was getting way too heavy to carry.

My actions gave him no choice but to agree to divorce. By the time we reached that point, the destruction I created could not be repaired. There would be no quick fix this time. We would divorce and go our separate ways except for the boys, and I would struggle with the situation I created. Honestly, the day the decree was signed made my list of the worst days ever, and I still shiver with fear when I think about it nearly thirty years later. I can recall it too clearly.

I woke up the next morning and regretted my decision and still do. My life went from the best days of bringing two boys into the world to another worst day ever because of my shame and fear.

Soon the good girl was gone, and the party girl with her self-preservation, don't-care-attitude, replaced her. Back and forth, the personalities shifted. It was all very exhausting. All this back and forth did was confirm every lie I believed. *You are NOT good enough. You are NOT worth loving. You are NOT_____ (fill in the blank).* What I really wanted was for the pain to stop.

The physical pain of abuse was excruciating but subsided in a couple of days. The internal pain gives birth to the death sentence. The abuse was the death of my identity. It was the erasure of who I was and who I wanted to be. Therefore, my identity was malleable. To survive, I was continually looking for ways to cope, bear the shame, and ward off the fear of being alone and unwanted.

Being alone was proof that I was not wanted and loveable. Being alone screamed that I WAS unlovable, unwanted, unattractive, unnecessary, all of those "un" words. Abuse does that. It catapults a victim from reality into a false reality painted by shame and fear and thousands upon thousands of lies whispered over and over by the enemy.

Wreckage

I am a word geek. I love words and their meanings, and I choose my words carefully when I explain my story, which is really God's story. I want to tell without a shadow of doubt the depth of the damage and height of His restoration.

The best way to describe what was left after I sabotaged and ended my marriage is wreckage. The dictionary defines the word as "the remains of something that has been badly damaged or destroyed."[4] That is the perfect description. Wreckage. Lives damaged. Marriage destroyed.

The worst part of my marriage's demise was the damage done to my children and to my ex-husband. Whatever the problem, whatever the brokenness, divorce is never, never the answer, not unless there is abuse of any kind. Never. The aftermath is not worth it. I'll admit some situations require divorce, such as domestic violence, but mine was not that situation. How different things could have been if it were not the damaged me that said, "I do." So different.

I left a trail of destruction when I ran away to New York and back home again. There were people hurt coming and going. I accept that responsibility and regret the pain I caused, but I could excuse it all on account of emotional scars—I pled insanity. But not with my children. Not with the heart of my husband. There is no excuse.

The wreckage left two boys growing up in the home of a step-father, not their own father. It left a man angry with the world and cynical, not living life. My shame was getting too heavy to bear. The pain was too excruciating to breathe.

As I have said, survival is the name of the game. What now? With a train wreck behind me, I had to face the fear of what was before me. I was alone, confirming my belief again that I was unlovable, unwanted, and so on. It was too difficult to think about, and I had two babies to care for. I laugh now because the only way I did survive was grace. Yes, I would continue to make bad choices, work overtime to numb the pain, and create more and more wreckage, but I would survive. It is by grace I have been saved from myself, not, definitely not, anything I did or could do.

Not too long after the divorce, I would love again and hope to be loved and fixed, and maybe emptied of my shame. My second husband would temporarily rescue me from the present fear. The storm would subside, for now, and calm be restored. I felt safe for a time. I would take a deep breath, exhale, and push the secret a little further down and kick the shame to the side awhile. Even rest my anxiety a little. I remember early in my second marriage naming my husband, "My Knight in Shining Armor." All I can say is, "Bless his heart." Again.

CHAPTER 6

Secret Sickness

Addictions

"Fake it till you make it." "Being a part of something is more important than being the center of attention." These are a couple of the numerous Alcoholics Anonymous truisms I heard and spoke for many years.

A truism is "a statement that is so obviously true that it is almost not worth saying." It is a statement or cliche that is obvious and self-evident. It is like having multiple mottos. As an attendee of Alcoholics Anonymous (A.A.), I learned a whole list of truisms were necessary to stay sober. These pithy cliches remind recovering addicts and alcoholics, like me, of truths they need to grasp to survive. Sometimes the easiest things to know are the hardest to remember.

How's that for a truism?

I believe the phrases, "Secrets make you sick," or "You are only as sick as your secrets," are the truest of the truisms. Secret sickness has many symptoms—emotional issues, no self-esteem, dangerous behavior, self-harm, and, most often, alcoholism and addiction.

The hardest truism to swallow, I found the one that is still diffi-cult for me to agree with is, "Once an addict (or alcoholic), always an addict (or alcoholic)." For me, addiction became the most obvious and

55

the latest symptom of my secret by the time I reached my mid-thirties. I attended more than a few A.A. meetings after a vacation at a faraway rehabilitation facility.

My shoulders slump, and my head hangs just considering the list of many shames.

Becoming an addict happened by accident. But really, that's how it always happens. Who sets out or makes a plan to be an addict? No one. Ever. But I did become an addict, adding the label to my already heavy coat of many shames. So far, my pockets are filled with the secrets of abuse, the damage and ruin of my marriage, and now, addiction, and alcoholism. That is in addition to the many smaller pebbles of shame secrets. To protect the innocent who will be unnamed, I can't even tell you everything. My shoulders slump, and my head hangs just considering the list of many shames.

Addiction didn't happen overnight. The enemy is a thief who prowls ready to devour his prey. He was waiting for the weakest link in my armor to fall loose so that he could push the arrow deeper. He watched and listened until I was comfortable. Then he added a heaping dose of family discord. "Boom!" He had the excellent opportunity to make the arrow burn.

Do Over

The path to addiction was a crooked road, and the first step was the end of my first marriage. Without knowing or intending it, my first husband triggered fear and shame in me. I can't pinpoint the exact event or words that started it, but fear and shame rose up. Perhaps he was angry at something I did or did not do. Or he could have been disappointed in the way I did something. It doesn't really matter. The only thing that mattered to my abuse-altered brain was to get away from any *possible* pain.

Always on the alert for possible pain or danger, I went into survival mode. Before he could end it with me, I ended it with him. I ran away—again. Of the fight, flight, or freeze, I fled that one. Our marriage ended after less than ten years.

When I met my current husband a few months later, he was everything my first husband was not. It was like starting over. A clean slate. A do over. I would get it right this time.

He was spontaneous and had no concern for what people thought or said about him. He loved to have a good time and surround himself with a lot of fun-loving people. Most of all, he made me feel safe and protected. He had my back. If I had a need, he met it. If someone or something threatened to ruin me, he took care of it. He did what I could not for myself and my children. He showered me with gifts and trips and lavish dinner dates. He was the knight, and I was the princess rescued from the tower.

We made it a habit of being spontaneous at all times. We took an oath to live without plans. The pendulum swung again.

Have you ever watched a pendulum? Not the Newton's Cradle of five silver balls you see on the desks of executives in movies and the sale rack at Sharper Image stores. No, a pendulum is a ball or arrowhead-shaped stone attached to a string. Add force of some kind, and the ball swings widely in the opposite direction. Eventually, the pendulum will come to the center again, but not until it turns wild and wide.

A more authentic picture of me is the pendulum swinging off the string and out of the ballpark. What made me go from good girl to party girl with such ease, again? It was a mixture of secrets covered in shame and fear. It was self-protection and hiding my true self. Leaving my good girl behind and putting on my party shoes again proved to me and everyone who knew me that I was not good enough.

I was a girl who wanted a good time. I could not be good. Part of me believed when I married my second husband that we would be divorced in no time. I was not a good wife, I believed. My first hint was during the wedding ceremony, when I put the ring on the wrong hand again. It must have been an omen.

For a time, it was wedded bliss—again. For a time. My husband remained my knight, standing between me and danger, wielding his imaginary sword against every perceived attack. Everything was perfect, and I felt safe.

After a year, we bought my dream house. It was big and beautiful, a bedroom for each boy, and five bathrooms. The day we moved in was a happy day. It was an excellent place for my boys to grow.

Within a year, we welcomed my baby boy number three. Again, I knew the heavenly joy of being wrapped in the indescribable comfort of hearing the cry of my newborn. Is there any way to bottle that feeling, that emotion, that comes when you hear your baby cry for the first time?

Fear, the what if's, pain, and danger are powerful motivators.

But the unrelenting fear and "what if's" controlled me, making my mind a scary place to live. Safely within the walls of my lovely home and the reassuring care of my husband, my thoughts bombarded me with fear of the worst. What if my husband decided he didn't need me? What if he did not like the way I cleaned the house or cooked? What if? What if? I worked myself into exhaustion to ward off the "what ifs." Every effort and ounce of energy was devoted to proving "what ifs" wrong. I would not give my husband fodder to change his mind about me. The foundation of my safety became my efforts. It was a false security, ready to tip any time. Always in survival mode. Fight, flight, or freeze.

Fear, the what if's, pain, and danger are powerful motivators.

There are so many things to fear. Heights? Spiders? Closed in spaces? When my address was on Easy Street, and I believed I had everything I needed, I let my worst fears run free. I told myself, "This is too good to be true." I began to imagine the hundreds of possible losses and I was sure I would not survive a single one.

The Bottom

The trouble with being perfect is that at some point, the only way to go is down.

After our beautiful third son was born, the struggle of a blended family overshadowed our happy home. It all started when my thirteen-year-old stepson came to live with us. He resented me (*hated* is probably a better word), and I resented him with equal venom for messing up our harmony. He was combative and went out of his way to make every single member of our household miserable. He succeeded admirably. On the other hand, I did not help matters by engaging in the war.

During those short three or four years, there was plenty of fault to go around. We all wanted our way, and our way did not include others.

Blended marriages can work and often do. However, blended families resulting from divorce on both sides under the wrong circumstances have a harder time succeeding. But I was determined to win this battle. My security was at stake.

Since we have been married for over twenty years, I guess you could say we won the war. However, the battles in between were horrific. Screaming, tears, slammed doors, locked doors, and anger all around—for everyone. With enough time, the turmoil became painful, so painful I sought to numb every nerve in my body and my brain. Three years of addiction turned into thirty days in rehab,

One of the worst things about keeping the secret of abuse is the pain.

a near-divorce twice, the loss of so many earthly comforts, and my worst nightmare coming true—losing the only love I really trusted, my children.

One of the worst things about keeping the secret of abuse is the pain. The very definition of a secret is that no one knows. If no one knows the secret, then they can't know the pain. Add turmoil from the outside, such as an unhappy blended family, and escaping all the emotions becomes the only goal. The aim is not to feel anything, not pain, anxiety, fear, resentment. Nothing.

I have used relationships, promiscuity, and food as numbing agents, but nothing numbs the heart and mind like narcotics. How I went from drinking too much to purchasing drugs is not essential. The critical point is that when I thought I controlled the drug, that's when I had no control.

It started small, recreational—only on the weekends when the boys were at their father's, and when our baby was with the grand-parents. But at the end of three years, I knew more about buying, using, and, at times, selling cocaine, than I should ever have known. There will be so many people who read this honest admission and turn away in judgment. I understand. I probably would as well. Just know that I am not who I was then. If you stick with me, you will see how God changes everything.

In three short years, I was a full-blown drug addict. But I felt nothing. *Nothing.* And that's just what I wanted—no pain, no love, no joy, no fear, no shame, nothing. I was a ghost, and in my mind, I deserved my situation. I did not belong anywhere good.

Black Sheep

To be a "black sheep" means to be "regarded as a disgrace or failure by his or her family or peer group."[2] A black sheep does not look like the others in the herd. A black sheep stands out, not because of beauty or accomplishment, but because she does not fit, there is something wrong with her.

I always felt like the black sheep in my family. From my abuse-driven imagination, I believed there was something wrong with me, while my younger brother and sister were pictures of perfection. They were successful college graduates, married to loving, successful spouses with perfect children, living in perfect houses. I compared myself and my circumstances to theirs, and the shame burned my cheeks.

On the other hand, I was divorced, with no college degree, a crazy angry home, and now I had become an addict. How much more of the outcast could I be? The lies in my head grew incredibly loud. I did not blame my family. I was different and felt like an outsider from the beginning. My impression was that I was an orphan adopted into a family that changed their minds, but it was too late to trade me in.

My abuse-damaged brain, continually in fear and survival mode and now altered by drugs, always proved what I believed people were thinking about me. In other words, I believed I was the black sheep, so I made it true.

I trusted the lie that my brother, sister, mother, and father all saw me as a failure. I was a failure at marriage, at education. I ran away to live with a man, and now I was using illegal drugs. They were so right, I told myself. If I were them, I wouldn't want me either. I would change my mind and send me back as well. Who could blame them? The lies were so loud I could not hear my family agonizing over my deep dive into the pit. My senses were not attuned to notice the truth.

After three years, hundreds of thousands of dollars, the decline of my health, and the extreme suffering of my children, my family intervened. With a drug-altered mind, I saw the effort as more proof that I was the black sheep, the outcast, the sister no one talked about. I thought they'd want to "send her away." And they did.

It's the shame, I tell you. Secrets and shame. Mix the two, and it's a lethal drink of self-loathing, self-destructing, vision-impairing, brain-altering poison. You can't stand yourself because of the secret, but you can't tell anyone because of the shame. Shame and secrets are a prison you commit yourself to and believe without a doubt that you deserve. Behind the bars of the prison, you are chained to the secret and the shame.

With my family's help, I spent thirty days in a rehab facility that I could not find on a map today. To this day, I still don't know where I was. I can't even remember the name of the facility. At the end of my stay, I was sober and clean for thirty days. I am sure it was the hangover haze of the drugs, but I cannot recall many details of rehab.

I do remember the facility was somewhat like a prison, only with comfortable beds and open windows. I could not shave my legs for a month because no razors were allowed in your room. And while I was there, one similarly suffering woman tried to kill herself in the bathroom with a broken makeup mirror. I guess that describes the people and the place. I was grateful for the end of drinking and drugs, but I would leave there and enter another kind of hell.

Nightmares

As the self-proclaimed black sheep, outcast, and now princess with a broken crown, I was more vulnerable than ever to fear and an "abuse" brain. When I came home from the rehab that I still can't clearly remember, my world was all upside down. My husband was gone. We lost our home, and my children lived with my mother. It was a mess. A huge, broken mess.

What I couldn't see clearly at the time was how much my family was hurting. My children were confused and afraid, their security and routine disrupted. Suddenly, they were living at their grandmother's house, not understanding why their mother disappeared. Only a toddler at the time, my youngest son has no clear memory of the months spent at my mother's house. My oldest son, on the other hand, was a teenager then, and he recalls me being "sickly" before I left for rehab. He was wise even then.

After I came home, my mother agreed to let me and the boys live with her until we got back on our feet, but there were stipulations. We—and by that I mean me—could stay as long as I did not return to my former situation. I agreed, half-heartedly. Among the many restrictions were regulations. I could not reconcile with my husband, had to attend regular A.A. meetings, and had to get a job. I mostly followed my mother's rules for a time. Mostly.

My husband and I met secretly. That's crazy, right? Meeting your husband secretly, so your mother doesn't know? I was caught in the middle. On one hand, I desperately wanted to please my mother and hopefully silence her judgement and disappointment. And on the other hand, he is my husband. We secretly stole time together trying to find our way back to sanity. That was until my mother discovered our rendezvouses. Why did I feel so wrong doing something so right? Crazy, right?

Since I did not meet the requirements of our agreement, my mother asked me to leave her home, and I did with my two oldest sons. My mother had temporary guardianship of my youngest son and she insisted he stay, and I had no choice.

When the intervention and rehab plans were birthed, I agreed to surrender temporary guardianship of my three-year-old son to my mother while I disappeared to rehab. Then, through a series of unfortunate missteps, my husband had to agree to the guardianship as well. He also had no choice.

The temporary guardianship was logical, right? In case she needed to take him to the doctor, right? Of course, it was just temporary, right? The two older sons' father did not feel the need to put the issue before the court. Even in my healing state, he felt it did more harm than good to take them away, too.

The guardianship of the youngest son was valid, according to the court. My mother, who I believe was acting out of fear and love, could keep my son when I left her home, and she did.

Remember that worst nightmare? It was materializing and my eyes were wide open.

There is evidence that about ninety-nine percent of our worst fears, or "what ifs," never happen. The one percent that do happen are the fears that kill you.

My worst nightmare was losing my children. The thought of a single son being taken away made me nauseous, and when the "one percent" became a reality it was as bad as I imagined. My young son lived with my mother for nearly a year. I was only allowed supervised visitation, which included trips to the park and meals out with my son and my supervisor, which was usually my mother. Many times, I was denied visitation.

There is no way to describe this pain. No words can competently describe the agony. It feels like a hollowness that grows and spreads until there is deep emptiness. The heartbreak washed over me in waves crashing over and over until I wanted to drown. So many nights, I laid myself across my mother's porch, sobbing so hard my body ached, begging to see and hold my son. So many tears. So many tears.

The courts eventually ended the guardianship. My husband and I proved to be clean and sober, and there was no basis for the guardianship. Reluctantly, and I do mean very reluctantly, my mother returned my son, his car seat and toys, then removed all contact for nearly two years. Christmases, holidays, birthdays celebrated as if I was an orphan—no word from my mother or my siblings. I was really the black sheep now. Even after my mother and I finally mended our relationship, we never spoke of those years. It's as if they never happened.

Redemption

My husband, three boys, and I moved away that same fall, away from the places that reminded me of the pain, the wrong choices, the places where I perpetrated my worst. We needed to start somewhere new, where no one knew the story.

We found a tiny rental house, much the opposite of the two-story, four-bedroom, four-bath house we lost to foreclosure. We five moved into three tiny bedrooms with old brown shag carpet, wood paneling in every room except the kitchen, which sported wallpaper from 1972. There was only one bathroom, but the spacious fenced backyard with towering pine trees made up for any inadequacies. The nearby schools were a plus as well.

The first days in our new home were difficult. When we moved in, we had nothing. We still owned a few pieces of furniture and our clothes, but the house did not come with a washer and dryer or a refrigerator. Nor did we have the funds to run to Lowe's and purchase one or two. There was nothing to do but wait until we could. So, we bought a big red ice chest where we kept the food and milk cold until a refrigerator magically appeared, and I regularly washed laundry at the laundromat. I pushed the ice chest in the gaping hole in the kitchen where a fridge should go. It looked so silly and out of place, but we were so happy to be as far away from the past as we could be and beginning to rebuild our lives. A lack of major appliances didn't matter.

The kids started school, and my husband's law practice was rebuilding. We were on the mend. I found a job at the school where my children attended, and we even regularly attended church. There was only one way to go from here: up. Everything was different now, I told myself. My inner self worked tirelessly to hide the past and deny problems and weak places in the armor. All that secret sickness was in the rearview mirror. Thirty days in rehab and nearly losing custody of my sons cured me.

One day I found myself alone at home, which rarely happened. I was probably cleaning the house, folding laundry, or something housewife-related. I recall catching sight of the red ice chest out of the corner of my eye. The house was small and made it possible to see the red ice chest from almost any room in the house. It was never entirely out of sight until I went to sleep. That day, I spied it, and emotions erupted and spilled out everywhere.

Maybe I wasn't so cured. The weight of my coat of shame remained heavy. The secret still laid hidden. My self-made prison chains rattled, and I suddenly felt the depth of what happened over the last three-plus years. I could see where I had been and where I was now. The past and pain was too much. I wanted to collapse, fold up, and disappear.

I dropped to my knees, leaning against the red ice chest, and, for the first time in a long time, I prayed. You know the Psalms where David is "crying out?" Well, this moment must have been the way he felt. Agony is not the right word, not even anguish. It felt like death calling out from deep within. The tears fell in a flood. Prostrate on the floor, I begged and pleaded with God to forgive me. I didn't deserve His mercy, but could He just help my children? Please, Father, be kind to my children. I deserve hell, but not them. I pleaded for help, for Him to take the awful pain, to show me a way out, and could He send a refrigerator? Because I didn't know how we would ever be able to afford one soon.

God answers prayers. A family friend called the next day and asked if we still needed a fridge, and yes, we did. Thank you, God. Our friends will never know how God used them to answer my desperate prayer.

Please know I do not want this to be my story. I am not pleased to be a recovering addict, divorced, and childhood sexual abuse survivor. I don't want any of it. I want the fairy tale with glass slippers and castles, but God had better plans for me. At that point, lying across the cooler in my tiny rental house, I was blind and could not see it, but God was preparing me for something bigger than I could dream.

And for my family, children, friends, and acquaintances reading my story, I don't want it for them. It is not a pretty story. I know. If I'm to have a story of childhood abuse, I want it to be about my family knowing when I was eleven and the perpetrator being punished. I want the story to be about healing before all of this madness could transpire. I want to be healthy, in my thoughts and choices and relationships. I don't want to live in fear and always in survival mode. I want to know I am lovable, wanted, and valuable. Isn't that what we all want?

After I stood up from the kitchen floor, all I wanted was Jesus. I dove headfirst into church, ministry, and worship. I soaked up every book, and attended every nearby Christian women's event. I studied Scripture and about Scripture, and, believe it or not, this girl with a crazy past even became the Sunday School teacher at our little church. Of course, not one person knew my history. Not one ever will, well, until they read this story. I wanted it that way. The person I was is dead and gone. The person I want to be is a work in progress.

After God gave us a refrigerator, He continued to bless us over and over. My children grew and flourished, God prospered us lavishly, and my marriage was at its fullest.

At the end of every fairy tale, it says, "They lived happily ever after." I really wish they could.

CHAPTER 7

New Vision

Fruit

After my meeting with God in the kitchen of our tiny rental house, I wanted to be part of everything that had to do with God. My "to do" list looked more like a list of mission projects than a list of my chores I was too busy to finish. I volunteered at the crisis pregnancy center, helped with Vacation Bible School, and attempted to grow a women's ministry (which was a Genesis flood-sized failure). I had my toe in every ministry project that was even whispered under a church roof.

"Hi, my name is Tammy, and I'm a mission project addict."

To find my fix, I frequently crashed mission projects at other churches; my own church backyard was not big enough. I desperately wanted God to know He did not make a mistake in blessing my family with a refrigerator and rescuing me from the pit I had dug for myself. I owed Him, and my debt was enormous. So, I had to get busy.

My first ever mission trip would send me overseas. Surely, a short-term international mission trip should pay off a big chunk of my debt to God, so I thought. Spreading the gospel far and wide would be worth a lot to God. I believed that what He wanted from me.

In addition to applying for a passport, I was required to share my salvation story with the pastor leading the excursion. In my most confident voice, I told him the "Reader's Digest" version. Not too much that he might reject my application, but just enough to let him know that God was working on me and in me to create a masterpiece. The pastor listened carefully as I tearfully told him the good stuff. The condensed version went something along the lines of, "I was saved at nine with my grandmother beside me."

"At sixteen, I began a prodigal lifestyle."

"I tried to fix my problem lifestyle on my own and failed in a bad way."

"Turned to drugs, and then Jesus rescued me."

The end.

I left out the whole abuse thing. Shame and fear convinced me sharing that part of my story meant that the pastor would reject me for sure. Who wants a broken, soiled, unworthy girl on their mission team?

At the end of my condensed life story, Mr. Pastor paused for a moment. It must have felt too long, because anxiety began to rise up in my chest, and I noticed that I was holding my breath.

I did not expect his response.

"The day in your kitchen is the day you were saved, not at nine years old." This was a telephone interview, but I imagined him leaning back in his chair, filled with the satisfaction of his spiritual diagnosis.

Did I hear him correctly? Was he saying that my "red ice chest" experience was actually my salvation story?

"But I was baptized and everything," I argued.

The pastor told me that my life up until the point of my encounter with Jesus in the kitchen was void of God. There was no fruit, he explained. And if my life did not show spiritual change—fruit—then Jesus was not in me.

He was right about one thing. There was no fruit.

With no fruit to show the pastor, I assumed he must be correct.

I fashioned the pastor's words into rocks shaped like shame and put them in my pocket. While I was abroad and for months after I returned, the pastor's words were on repeat in my head. "There was no fruit." To me, this translated to "no value." No fruit, no value.

If Mr. Pastor's words were true, then all those lost years, those prodigal days, were a waste. I survived on my own, abandoned by even God. God was not present, nor was Jesus, or the Holy Spirit to guide me. In other words, I was dead. How could that be?

Prison

Was it just dumb luck that I survived? What about that time I tried to end my life in the tenth grade? Was God not there to rescue me? Or, that time I walked away unharmed when I stumbled out of a bar in Spanish Harlem. Was it not God's mercy that saved me? Or, that time I almost overdosed on a cocaine binge. Did I rescue myself? Or, did God rescue me from the edge of death so many times? It had to be God.

If Mr. Pastor was right, that God was not present until I surrendered my life while lying over an Igloo ice chest, I reasoned that because of my past, it could also be true that not even God could love me. No God. No love. No God. No worth.

I shared this heartbreak with April very near the time I told her my secret about abuse.

"Even God couldn't love me," I told her. My mother and father did not love me. The people who used and abused me did not care about me. How could they? I was not worthy of love. Not even God could love me. Was my shame too much for Him? I needed to know. Was I so lost, that even God could not find me? I questioned everything my shallow understanding of God possessed. Was I more than God could handle? Were my sins so dark Jesus' blood couldn't cover me?

April asked me to describe the shame that I believed God struggled to remove. I closed my eyes. In my mind, I could see a prison void of any comfort. There were bars of a cage surrounded by a damp stone cell. A sliver of light burst through a tiny crack between the stones. There was enough light to allow me to see the ugliness where I existed and also understand there was no escape. Tears fell as I considered how people would react if they could see me in the cell, if they knew my secrets and what I had done. Were they laughing as they walked past the cage? Were they tossing stones at the ugly monster doomed to wither away?

That's what my shame from abuse felt like. A cage within a prison with no hope of escape.

That's what my shame from abuse felt like. A cage within a prison with no hope of escape.

The anxiety choked, and I recall closing my eyes, picturing my prison, and describing the details for April. How could I ever be free? How would I know freedom?

I needed a key to open the door to freedom.

The Key

With the overseas mission trip behind me, I continued to wade through the possibility that I had been alone in my past, that I was lucky to have survived the previous four decades—not carried by God like I had believed. The only thing I knew for sure was that in the present, Jesus was with me, but even that knowledge seemed fragile. Maybe that's why seeing the face of my abuser on social media slammed the shame-prison door and turned the lock.

Still teetering on the possible reality that in those years before meeting Jesus in my kitchen, I survived without the hand of God, I saw my abuser's face and remembered why I was chained to shame. My faith was fragile, and I was ready to give up this Christian thing. I wasn't good at it anyway. And when I looked into his social media eyes, it was over. His face was a solid confirmation to my trauma brain that I was shameful and not lovable. Give up and get out.

Combine the doubt of my Christianity with the cold stare of my first abuser, and I believed there was no reason to keep going. The weight of my shame became too much to bear another moment. I needed it to stop. My heart, mind, and body longed to silence the punishing voices and find permanent rest. The pain was too much. Was that the key I longed for? Death?

Or could the key to freedom be me standing atop the highest peak and screaming as loud as I could? As loud as it was necessary for the whole world, my whole world, to hear, "I was raped!" I would scream and scream and scream if I could. Over and over until someone heard me. Yet I had no voice. Shame and fear stripped me of the words. The tornado swirled in my head until I knew my arms and legs and head would be pulled in opposite directions. There was no air to breathe, no escape from the cage, no hope.

If there is a lock or a prison door, there must be a key. The key to my freedom existed, I was sure, but I had no ability to see it.

I imagined a ring with hundreds of keys dangling and clanking, each one opening a lock to a door. The key I needed was surely suspended on that ring. One key was all I needed, the one that opened my shame-prison door. With that door open, all the other locks would fall open.

The key was right there within reach. But which key? Each of the many keys was the answer to open a door to a closet, or the gate to a garden, or a prison cell. The solution was to choose the right key. There were many, and what if I chose wrongly? I had already tried so many wrong solutions and keys, and none fit, often only twisting the lock tighter.

Running away, being anyone I needed to be, drugs, alcohol, promiscuity, and actions I don't have pages enough to share—these keys did not fit the lock. Where and what was the key, for God's sake?

Was it so simple as telling the secret?

I have always wanted to tell the secret. I wanted to tell my mother and father, but I was more afraid of their disappointment. I feared upsetting the balance. As a little girl and well into my adulthood, I believed it was my responsibility to keep everyone calm and happy. And not tell the secret.

I wanted to tell my grandmother, but I feared I would not be "her girl." I could be replaced. I wanted to tell someone, but I didn't have the words. I wasn't sure what had happened and feared it was my fault and I would be punished either with pain or withdrawal. So I kept the secret.

The secret wanted to be unleashed so many times. With no voice and no language to describe what happened, I just never had the courage to utter the words. I wanted to so many times and came very close, but at the last second inhaled the words and the prison door closed again. And I hid the secret deeper.

There were one or two people whom I believe suspected I hid a secret. In high school, not too long after the abuse and molestation, there was a teacher who seemed to see right through my mask. She knew something in me was tangled and broken. She even asked me if there was something I needed to talk about. Fear said, "No. I'm fine. There is no problem."

Then again in my first writing class in college, I wrote a personal narrative about the bus driver who groomed me, used me, and taught me to be quiet. I think the title was something like, "They Could Never Know." When the instructor returned my essay, I found her comments written in blue ink in the margin, "Thank you for sharing this painful story." I denied it was a real story. "It was fiction," I said. "I'm fine. There is no problem."

Locked away in a prison of my design, chained to shame that was not mine, and believing lie after lie about my identity in Christ, I could not take another breath. I didn't want to. I needed a key.

"Try counseling," God said while a storm swirled on the horizon.

So I did, and through hours and hours of time with April, I found the key.

The key to freedom was telling.

Freedom

When I spoke the words of my secret, I was free. When the secret was no longer a secret, I was free. The split second I uttered the words, "I was raped when I was eleven," there was no secret to hold me captive, and I was free.

The damp stone walls encircling the cage crumbled. The light now illuminated everything, especially freedom.

With April's help and God's strength, I told the story to others. Each time I uttered the words, my voice grew stronger. The more I told the story, the freer I became. My coat of many pockets weighed down with pebbles and rocks of shame lightened. The more I spoke, the more my pockets were emptied.

The more I told the story, the freer I became.

Secrets and shame cannot exist out in the open. Shame from secrets thrives in the darkness, and the deeper the secret is hidden, the stronger it becomes. Name it, tell it, bring it out of the dark, and it shrivels and shrinks, and its power is gone.

With each person who heard, my voice grew more distinct and formidable, and the shame shrank and withered until it cowered in the corner of the prison I escaped. That could not have happened until I told the first person.

At first, talking about my childhood trauma was awkward, and perhaps I was a little too enthusiastic. Going from zero to one hundred can be dangerous.

My first opportunity came when a church asked me to speak to a group of about 200 teenage girls. I volunteered at the local crisis pregnancy center, which made me available to represent the center. The topic of the event was purity and knowing how much God values each girl. We are His masterpiece. The church did not ask me to tell my story of sexual abuse and a battle with shame. The coordinators did not know my story. What they wanted was a gut honest presentation that encouraged girls to choose purity. What better way to scare them straight than a retelling of forty years of promiscuity, drugs, and dreams of suicide? Right?

My life details may not have been the best way to illustrate God's will for purity, but I told the story anyway. There was much squirming on the front pew, mostly adults. I believe I lost the girls somewhere about five minutes in when I described being lured into a neighbor's house. To them, my story was probably no worse than what they see on television or social media. Unless, of course, it had also happened to them. I'll admit, I may have been too excited to tell the details and forgot to focus on the God part.

What I learned from that moment was that my story, any story of God's rescuing, redeeming, and restoring power, is sacred and best spoken to give Him glory. My motive was to prove that I had the courage to say the words out loud. Point proven. The church never asked me back again.

My children, the boys, were the next to hear the truth.

The most difficult to tell was the first.

"I need to tell you something," I began.

Silence on the other end of the phone. Oldest son could not see me, but I was shaking, quivering, unable to speak for a moment. Thankfully, I practiced what I would say. My goal was to stay on topic.

"When I was eleven, I was raped." I said in slow motion.

I told how when I was eleven, the neighbor boy lured me into his house on a hot summer afternoon and my life, the person I was, changed.

"Momma," he always called me. "I am so sorry."

He asked more questions, and I was willing to answer them all. This was a turning point in our relationship, a watershed moment. He was already an adult, our history made, but this truth would change the way he saw me and give him a new perspective on our past.

Before I told my son, I pictured in my mind how it could play out. He could choose not to believe me, which would be the worst. Or he could be embarrassed and ashamed of me and never see me again, which is still fairly bad. Or he could accept me the way I am and love me anyway. Which he did. What he does not know is that

his acceptance melted away another layer of shame. Shame shared
is shame gone.

Being the action-oriented son he is, he also needed names and
possible locations. He wanted justice. I explained, "It's too late. He
died early in the year. Justice is now God's."

I told my middle son and youngest back-to-back. Their responses
are treasure as well. The middle son listened and nodded when I
finished the same speech I gave the first son and simply said, "That
explains everything." He understood me now. All of the decisions and
coping mechanisms made sense. My introspective son now understood
me. The shame melts again.

Baby son lived at home when I told him. I was afraid he would
be the one who did not understand. He simply said, "Nothing you
say will change the way I see you." I could feel the shame melt and
disappear.

Telling my sister was probably the hardest. Because of my tumultuous past, she and my brother suffered direct hits from my bad
behavior. They watched as I self-destructed as a teen and ran away.
The two of them saw how drugs and alcohol nearly destroyed me,
my children, and my home. It was my sister and brother who came
together to intervene and place me in rehab. Our relationship was
rocky, and only in the past few years has it been restored. I feared
telling her the most. It would be one more tragic episode she would
endure. I feared losing our relationship.

I was wrong. She has been my strongest supporter. Can you see
the shame disappearing?

It was a while before I told my brother. Every time we were
together, it was a holiday or vacation or some happy event. When I
told him, I did not want his memory of that event to be me telling
him I was raped when we were kids. So, I told him when our father

was dying. No joke. He will remember one or the other, my story or our father.

A little bit of shame disappears each time I can tell the truth of my story, the story of how I was raped at eleven, molested by a trusted bus driver, and traveled a prodigal road that left me locked away in shame. Telling brings the shame and secret into the light where it must die.

Telling brings the shame and secret into the light where it must die.

It would be naive to believe that everyone who hears my story will respond in the same loving way my sons, sister, and brother did. No, the reality is someone will not believe me or try to convince me it was my fault. I will not be able to see who they are in advance so I can avoid them. I will be devastated at first and feel the sting of shame for a moment. It must be easier for those people to not believe my story than to believe my story.

But now I know how telling is the key to removing that shame. I have the key. If I come across someone who calls me a liar or pins the blame on me, I'll find someone else to listen. Maybe that someone needs to hear my story so they can tell their story, too. Then my shame and their will wither. Shame will not thrive in the light.

And, Mr. Pastor, no disrespect, but God was with me, in me, and for me while I lived in darkness. He saw me in the wilderness and stood beside me when I wanted to die. He stretched out his hand that held the key to freedom. He waited for me to see it and hear Him whisper, "try counseling." He knew me before I fully knew Him. I am the firstfruit of His rescuing love.

CHAPTER 8

Telling

Disappearance

Walking around wearing a coat laden with stones picked up and added to the pockets each time I experienced shame, bad choices, and regret weighs heavily on self-image and, in due time, relationships. The two are intrinsically tied. How I see myself affects how I live in relationships. If I see myself as unlovable and unworthy, I am guarded and closed off, even with my children and husband. My imagination is filled with lies. They can't love me, I believe, especially if they knew my secret. My energy is spent hiding secrets and shame, not on nurturing relationships.

If I see myself as valuable and loved, I can take chances, be vulnerable, and trust others. My resources are used to build relationships, not avoid them. The key, then, was to rid myself of this uncomfortable coat of shame and tell the secret. And when I did, my improved self-view changed and, in turn, changed relationships. The secret had to be told.

The BBC's nostalgic television series, *Call the Midwife*, is a favorite binge-watch choice for me. I have lost whole weekends watching hours of nuns and midwives deliver babies and impart wisdom amid the setting of London's mid-century blue-collar suburb. At the time of this writing, during a pandemic quarantine, there are nine seasons available on Netflix, and I have seen all nine—three times.

During a recent weekend binge, one of the character's lines pierced me. Speaking with another younger nun of Nonnatus House, the aging nun and midwife, Sister Monica Joan, who was often mistaken for feeble-minded, said, "When a secret weighs heavily, we imagine it's our burden alone, but the opposite is true. Once it is spoken, it disappears."[1] Words of wisdom, for sure.

The question changed from how I keep the secret to how I live free of the secret.

When a secret is told, it disappears. When the secret is told, the shame diminishes. With no secret, I no longer had anything to hide from—no obstacle between me and freedom. The question changed from how I keep the secret to how I live free of the secret. What is life without a mask to hide my shame? What does it look like without the fear of people's judgment? How do I navigate through relationships being who I truly am? How do I guard against hurt and harm? How do I live with the knowledge that God loves me? How do I walk with my head up, knowing I am worthy of love because God loves me?

The answers to these questions did not come all at once, and in all honesty, I continue, like most survivors, to grasp the reality of the answers. April and I spent hours working to retrain my brain to think in a healthy way instead of through the filter of trauma, shame, and secrets. And the problem did not lie entirely in keeping the secret so long. These thoughts and lies that I believed about myself and the trauma of abuse rewired me. My brain rewrote the truth, and that truth became me.

The rewiring of my brain is not an excuse. Science shows that trauma disrupts and rewires healthy thinking into fear thinking. Until I could unravel the secrets and shame, my thoughts were framed by fear and shame. My mind needed retraining before I could live genuinely free. My mind needed rewiring to see life through freedom instead of shame. Labels I gave myself had to be removed and replaced. I needed truth to replace the lies I believed.

Ridding Out

Once upon a time, I participated in a women's Bible study that explained it this way: Our mind is equivalent to a "thought closet," where we store memories and experiences that guide the way we talk to ourselves.[2] The thoughts hanging in my closet ruled the words I said to myself.

The trauma of abuse and my life's origin caused me to tell myself that I was not worth love or even respect. I was shameful. There was something wrong with me.

Each time I thought about myself and who I was to God in this negative way, I hung a lie in my "thought closet." Over time, the negative thoughts filled the closet and pushed out the truth. My thought closet bulged with views shaped by shame and fear and lies. To retrain my brain, I needed to do some spring cleaning, purge my closet, and replace those thoughts with truth.

And isn't cleaning out the closet so satisfying? There is a deep feeling of gratification when all the clothes that don't fit or have passed their usefulness exit the premises. Seeing the worn out or regretful fashion choices hanging at eye level or, worse, scattered on the closet floor gives me great anxiety. I call this glorious process "ridding out."

Ridding out gives room for new beautiful things to wear to fill the closet. Items that fit and flatter. In the same way, clearing out the clutter of lies and hurtful self-talk in my thought closet makes room for God's amazing grace, mercy, and truth. These are things that fit better than shame, fear, and secrets.

The first thought or belief about myself that needed destroying was that something was wrong with me. I remember the day I sat in April's office and first spoke the words, "Nothing is wrong with me." The words felt uncomfortable, as if I was watching and hearing a stranger say them.

"Are you sure that's right?" I asked April. "I mean, I am sitting in a counselor's office working through shame and abuse. Are you sure there is nothing wrong with me?" I argued.

"Say it again," April encouraged.

"Nothing. Is. Wrong. With. Me."

As I repeated the words over and over, those five words began to fit better. Out with one lie, in with the truth.

When my youngest son was small, he participated—reluctantly—in church programs and school choir. He hated it and would often simply move his lips. He was probably mouthing, "Watermelon, watermelon, watermelon." That's what you do when you want to appear as if you are joining the chorus, yet you are silent.

Before each program, I reminded him to sing "loud and proud." That phrase became a mantra when he was unsure about himself. "Say it loud and proud," I would remind him. "I can do this. I am smart enough," he would shout when he was unsure and feeling like not enough.

I am fearfully and wonderfully made. I am chosen before the foundations of the earth. God created me, and nothing is wrong with me. Say it loud and proud.

These truths are true because God says they are.

Importantly, these truths are not the truth because I want them to be. These truths are true because God says they are.

God says I am fearfully and wonderfully made. God says I am chosen before the foundations of the earth. Each utterance pushed out one more lie hanging in the closet. These truths, sewn together, became a new coat with no pockets to hold shame and fear. These truths began to hang in my thought closet at eye level.

Practice

Cleaning out the thought closet did not happen overnight. Some days I felt uncomfortable trying to believe I was fearfully and wonderfully made. If "fearfully and wonderfully made" was a new pair of jeans, they didn't fit. It seemed like I was wearing someone else's clothes. The old things I believed about myself kept showing up. If my husband was upset with me, I retracted in fear and told myself I deserved his anger and perhaps even worse. If my sister did not answer my texts, I struggled with the fear that she did not want me. Old lies, thoughts and beliefs could quickly creep back into the thought closet. They were familiar, and often I did not notice when they popped up.

The things I told myself over the years and returned to all too often were not attractive, but they were comfortable.

These destructive thoughts fit like old shoes, similar to the pair of old running shoes at the bottom of my real clothes closet. I don't run anymore, but I hang on to them because they are familiar, comfortable, and easy to put on. They have been places with me. Those shoes and I have covered many miles, and, along the way, I tripped in a few potholes.

The shoes no longer have adequate support, and, if I wear them too long, they make my shins and legs ache. But I hang on to them, although they are of no use. Who knows, I might start running again or need a pair of "yard shoes."

The same is true of the words I spoke to myself for more than four decades. The words are familiar and comfortable, although I don't need them anymore. "Who knows, I might need that shame again," said no one ever.

It was no problem to tell myself that I deserved the worst because I am the worst, because it was a familiar thought. No effort, no energy was exerted to retell this lie. It was more challenging to put on the truth that I was loved, loveable, and worth true words.

But I must not give up on replacing lies with truth. It takes practice and vigilance. If I did take up running again, I would need new shoes and practice, running just a little at first. Over time, my endurance would grow and I could run longer and faster. Similarly, it takes practice and persistence to replace "old talk" for "truth talk."

The difficulty exists where the enemy lives— in my mind—and his battle plan is to attack when I am down.

Practice is a must because the battle to end the lies of shame is constant. This struggle will continue until I see Jesus where there is finally no pain or tears. Here in this world, the battle to transform my view from worthless to priceless rages on in this broken person.

Circumstances, difficult times, trials, and tribulations of just being alive can send my mind down a path I do not want to tread again. The difficulty exists where the enemy lives—in my mind—and his battle plan is to attack when I am down. All he needs is one tiny toehold of a shame lie to send me reeling toward the edge and back into captivity. He rattles the chain, waiting to ensnare my mind.

Capturing these shame-born thoughts takes practice and grace. It's like any muscle group that I need to strengthen—practice, practice, practice. No athlete gets it right every workout or crosses the finish line without setbacks. So, I need grace, both from God and myself.

Some battles are lost, but ultimately victory comes. I may not get it right every day or with every thought, but someday I will.

Changing my thoughts and beliefs about who I am changed my relationships as well. I had nothing to hide now. For the first time in fifty years, I was bare before the world and felt like I wasn't afraid of people looking at me. I was wearing new clothes this time, specially made by God.

In the beginning, putting on the new clothes of freedom from shame was like walking in six-inch spike heels for the first time. I was wobbly and lacking balance. I liked who I was in the mirror more each day, and I wanted everyone dear to me to see the same. This transparency meant my inner circle—children, family, and closest friends—encountered a different, new "Tammy." Often, people seemed to meet me for the first time. The protection of the mask faded, and my friends and family could see me, the real me.

With a growing positive self-image, my closest relationships began to change and grow, but other relationships struggled. Renegotiating these relationships was not without difficulty. Some close relationships moved to a whole new level of love and respect. Without fear between me and those who are dear, I was free to be vulnerable and open, ask questions, and tell truths.

But other relationships needed new boundaries—mostly, boundaries about where I could go and where I could not. When a relationship thrives on the dysfunction of shame and fear, it starves when the shame and fear is withdrawn. If that relationship is determined to live on shame and fear, sometimes it tries to grow what it needs. Sometimes people try to give us shame and make threats to keep us in fear.

In my case, I had to draw a line and say, "I want to have a relationship with you, but without taking on shame and fear." Without the food it needed to survive, some of these relationships shriveled and went out kicking and screaming. Meaningful connections, like those with my children and sister and brother and other family, deepened and flourished.

My connections with my children changed immeasurably for the better and for this I am the most grateful. For most of their childhoods, my boys watched me traverse life with a mask, hoping to hide my shame. Shame makes being fully present as a parent, friend, sister, wife, whatever the role, almost impossible. The energy used to protect my secret was costly. The boys witnessed long bouts of depression, addiction, anger, and events I am uncomfortable describing. What they experienced gives me great regret. I wanted to be the excellent mother they needed and deserved, but shame and secrets told me I would never reach that bar. And as is the way of shame, I became what I did not want to be.

Shared

When the secret is shared, it disappears, as Sister Monica Joan said.

As I mentioned before, my middle son's first words after learning the secret were, "That explains everything." Transparency and vulnerability with my boys freed me to build our relationships more than hiding a secret and left me open to be part of their lives without fear.

I remember the oddest emotions when my middle son was the first to get married. I was hyper-aware of the transition in our relationship, and the feeling was bittersweet. Our relationship was going to the next level—from mother and son to mother and married, adult son. I did not feel scared or hurt by the transformation, but a mix of peace, excitement, and as if I had just completed the most beautiful journey. I wonder if God feels that way when He watches His children grow. My sweet son moved from being my little boy, my teenage son, my college-kid son, and, in a way, my responsibility to the husband of my beautiful daughter-in-law. He belongs to her now.

The sweet part of that change was realizing he was not leaving me because of who I thought I was—a shameful person—but because of who he is. My heart was not broken because I believed he was leaving me because I was not worthy of his love. He was not choosing someone else over me. No. He did not move away to get away from me, which was what shame and fear convinced me was true—that everyone wanted to get as far away from me as possible.

He was moving on because he had discovered what love is.

If I had never told my son the truth about the secret, at that moment when he said, "I do," I would have missed the sweetest moment a mother of a son could experience—the transition in our mother-son relationship. I would have been spending my energy protecting my secret and hiding the shame, believing I was unloved and unwanted. I am so grateful for the opportunity to witness my sweet son marry a beautiful, godly woman and begin a beautiful, godly life with her without the secret between us.

The connection with my oldest benefited in the same way because of what I experienced with his brother. I witnessed my oldest son marry and felt the same bittersweet elation I felt before. Like Mary, I treasured these moments with my sons in my heart. My job as "momma" was done. My oldest now belongs to my second amazing daughter-in-law now.

I enjoy this newfound freedom with my sons. When I can spend time loving them, engaging in their lives, and being intentional building our relationships, I am the happiest. And when the youngest marries, I'll enjoy the same cherished moments as I did with the first two sons. I will treasure them in my heart.

Lines

Setting new relational boundaries gave me a challenge. Boundaries are where the other person stops, and I begin. It's where I draw the line between the other person and me.

I don't see it as a demand, like, "You cross this line, and we are at war."

No. It's more like, "I hear you, and I see you, but I can't give you what you are asking of me." Believing I was worthy of drawing a line where I began and others stopped was almost as freeing as telling the secret.

Setting boundaries was a step toward knowing that I was worth something. It meant I had choices. Drawing lines means I do not have to take on and internalize the unhealthy expectations of others. I could say no, or yes, but it was my choice. I could say no and walk away, not feeling as if something was wrong with me. I was me, and, for the first time in decades, I did not have to become what others wanted me to be to know love and be seen. This was truly new territory.

Think of boundaries as safety fences keeping the good in and the not so good out. Boundaries are not a bad thing. Quite the opposite. Abuse takes away your voice, your power, and your boundaries. That was the reason it was so easy to fall into promiscuity and addiction. I had no boundaries. If I did have lines, they were placed by the other person in the relationship. I belonged to everyone and everything. Remove the shame and the damaging self-talk, and boundaries pop up everywhere.

I learned to say no loud and proud without fear of the consequences. In the past, I said yes when I meant no and let myself be manipulated into doing things I regretted. Without working so hard to hide a secret, I was free to find my strength and voice to draw lines. In most cases, good relationships were strengthened.

The relationship with my mother and father was probably the hardest to reorganize. I lived and thought like a little girl for so long, even though I was a middle-aged mother of grown children. The outside did not match the inside. I feared my parents into adulthood—probably still do a little. In my head and heart, my job was to maintain the balance. I was responsible for keeping the peace, doing everything in my power to keep my father's anger at bay and keep my mother from withdrawing her love and attention.

When the secret was bare, and the shame was gone, I had to learn a new way of relating to my parents. I had to grow up. No longer acting out of fear and gradually understanding my worth, I was now free to say, with respect and love, of course, what needed to be said. It seemed like crazy talk at first, being an adult with my mother and father.

The first time I noticed a shift from child-me to adult-me happened over one holiday season. The pressure of holiday get-togethers fractures everyone's nerves. Being part of a blended family brings those nerves to the very end. Once I remarried, there were new holiday rules and even more stress. My mother insisted on a Christmas Eve celebration, and my mother-in-law insisted on the same. How can a woman, her three children, a stepchild, and a husband be in two places at the same time? Not possible, but weakened by shame, possessing no boundary vocabulary, and trying to keep the peace, I tried. Each year was full of tears and stress where opening gifts made me angry and the feast left me with heartburn. That was, until I found my voice and made a choice.

One year, I held my ground, and, at the breaking point, I lovingly explained that we would not be attending both dinners as a family. Instead, our bunch would be alternating time on Christmas Eve between the two families. There was a lot of push back. Even my husband was a bit bewildered.

The decision was not well-received at first from either side, but when there was half the stress and double the holiday cheer, everyone settled into a new routine. Under shame, I would have continued to be in two places at once making nightmares, not memories. According to the lies of shame, I did not deserve boundaries or choices. Without shame, I valued the happiness of my family and myself over pleasing people.

My marriage grew deeper and stronger without shame, too. When I was first married, I believed that I had to earn a place in the relationship. My duty was to clean the house, care for the children, maintain a job outside the home, and meet my husband's expectations. These are all true of a devoted wife and mother. These are all worthy pursuits of a wife and mother...but not when they are done as payment.

But my motivation, and the motivation of most survivors, is to earn love.

In a relationship of love and respect, a wife wants to display that kind of devotion and love. But my motivation, and the motivation of most survivors, is to earn love. Shame says I am not good enough for my husband's love, so I must work hard to earn it and keep it. In my relationship with Jesus, I saw myself as shameful and unworthy, so I had to participate in every mission opportunity. I had to earn His love. If I did not perform well enough, He could not love me. If the dishes were left in the sink, my husband would not love me.

Once you know your worth, the worth that God assigns, whether you struggle to grasp it or not, earning love seems less profitable. Without shame around my neck, I was allowed to say, "I am worth your love whether I wash another load of laundry, prepare another meal, or mow the yard. I am loveable." Some days I still struggle to grab hold of that truth. That, however, does not change the reality. Without shame and secrets, caring for our home became a gift—a gift of love and respect. Now, doing what I really don't enjoy, but know needs to be done, is an act of "we are in this together." If I don't sweep, mop, and shine the furniture, I am still worthy of love.

Friends

Once shame disappeared, acquaintances turned into deep friendships, and that transformation elated me. As a little girl, I dreamed of living in a neighborhood where my best friend lived two houses down. Our children would attend the same school, and our husbands would watch football together. I desperately wanted friends, real friends. What I pictured, I think, was me without shame and secrets. What would life be without those shame rocks in my pocket? In my little girl world, it meant friends who accepted and cared about me. Friends who never left because they discovered my secret.

Instead of weighed down by shame and wearing a mask to cover it, relationships only ever existed on the surface. I dreamed of girlfriends I could sip coffee with and tell my troubles to. Instead, I shared just the good stuff, the good girl. With shame disappearing and the secret floating around in the world, friend-

ships came. Not at first. I was guarded and skeptical. What sane woman wanted to be my real friend? It turned out, women with secrets!

There are women everywhere walking around with a secret.

There are women everywhere walking around with a secret. There are sisters in every circumstance who have secret abuse, secret hurt, secret addictions, secret relationships, and secret dreams. These women live on my street, attend my church, and shop at the same grocery store. Telling my secret, exposing my shame, led me straight to friends who need me as much as I need them.

I need friends and neighbors like that.

I give up on the Donna Reed dream. I am trashing the visions of fashionably-dressed, attractive women sitting in coffee shops chatting over lattes about their problems. I am on a search for women like me, healing from secrets and shame—or wanting to. I want neighbors and friends who understand when I call and say, "I'm not feeling the truth today." And they remind me of the truth. I need friends who carry tissues because they know I will need them once in a while. I want to be that friend who can honestly say, "I know how you feel." There is no better person to understand and empathize with my scars than a woman with similar scars. As Fred Rogers asked every week on his show for kids, "Won't you be my neighbor?"

CHAPTER 9

Rescued

Dreams

The most devastating pain of shame and secrets is a broken relationship with God. All other broken connections, such as with my family and my children, would mend even if I kept the secret. We could talk it out, make changes, and commit to repairing the break. But I feared the connection with God could not heal. I hoped that God did not know the secret nor see my shame. Maybe if I stayed far away from God, He wouldn't see what happened and what I had done to hide my shame.

For too many years, the shame stood between me and God like an impenetrable stone wall. As long as the secret of abuse remained in the dark, my relationship with my Creator felt disconnected. Shame convinced me that I was too ugly for even God to look at, which left me aching. We all have that longing that can only be filled with God.

The pain was not a hurting pain, like a stab wound or broken bone, but a longing that comes from deep, deep inside where you hide things. It's an epic emptiness that aches endlessly. Drugs, alcohol, and a litany of other painkillers cannot diminish it.

When I was deep in the throes of secrets and shame, I could not put a name on the emptiness, but I could feel it. I could feel the hopelessness in my stomach, an empty feeling, like I had not eaten all day, leaning toward nausea. I think it's the feeling of hopelessness combined with the fear that the pain and ache will never end. Until I told the secret, I believed I would always feel this way.

The pain of abuse and the resulting shame became so embedded in my being that I was sure my life would never be right, ever. Not as long as I hid secrets and bore shame. But, on the other hand, I could never tell the secret. I was trapped in a circle. My heart knew it was doomed to chase freedom from my secret and shame and find it nowhere. I wanted to be good enough for God to love, but I kept messing up, so I gave up. I wanted to know Jesus again, but there was no clear reason He would want to know me, so I told myself He did not. Knowing God was a dream. Being loved by God and being pain free felt like a fairytale.

And the fairytale goes something like this: Once upon a time, a nine-year-old little girl was sitting next to her grandmother in church. On that day, she glimpsed Jesus and freedom from sin, love, and acceptance. She felt no shame and hid no painful secrets. The day was a moment so far away and unreal. But the little girl's dream would be shattered by evil, rape, and sexual abuse. Too afraid to tell the world, she hid the secret and secrets birthed over and over. She took on the back-breaking weight of shame and clothed herself in its heaviness. With the shame too much to carry, she locked herself away in a dark, damp, cold prison and lived with the secret that she was too scared to share. The love she knew, the Savior she glimpsed, and the relationship with God, appeared gone. Would she ever be rescued? Would the little girl ever know freedom? Is there a happily ever after?

Shame and its sister, Secrets, shattered every dream and fairytale story. Their power convinced me that God did not and could not love me. It was all a hopeless dream.

Sometimes little tidbits of Scripture would float across my mind. "For God so loved the world…" Yes, He does, but He meant everyone else, not me. There was no way God loved me, I told myself. If He loved me, then why would He let rape happen to an eleven-year-old little girl just out for a ride on her bike. Why, God?

The first time I considered the question of how a good God could let abuse happen to a little girl, I wondered why God let something so damaging, so traumatizing, so painful occur. Why would God allow a little girl who gave herself to Jesus to be drawn in by evil disguised as kindness? Why would a sovereign God, who created the universe and is all-powerful, allow a teenage boy to do what he did?

I can't answer all of those questions. Only He can, and He will.

I can say that when it happened, I thought it was because He did not want me or see me. I was shameful, of course. Dirty, ugly, and something was wrong with me.

"You were wrong about Jesus," the shame whispered. "He can't love you," it lied. As long as I lived under shame, a relationship with Jesus and knowing God loves me remained unfathomable, unreal, and non-existent. Everyone else could know Jesus and pray to God, but not me.

But I was wrong.

When my secret was told and taken out into the light, the wall began to crumble.

God never ended our relationship. He never turned away or covered His eyes because of my shame. Once I told the secret and began to release shame and get help to heal the wounds of abuse, I was able to look back over the years of prodigal living and see God everywhere. He never abandoned me. With each step of my life, each turning point and milestone moment, He was there rescuing me. When I was promiscuous, He was there. When I used cocaine and when I begged to die, He was present. He was there watching and waiting to rescue me.

I thought God had abandoned me and left me to suffer. My friends and family, at times, turned away, mostly when I was at my worst. Who could blame them? But God remained. He was right beside me, watching and waiting to reach out and rescue me when I was about to go under for the last time. God waited for me to step off into the deep end of the pool so He could rescue, redeem, and restore our relationship.

Perhaps

But why would a good God let me live in a shame prison for over four decades? I began to think of the maybes. Maybe because it is His plan. But how could this be? Perhaps...

He didn't let me stay where I was. The enemy deceived me into believing I deserved the prison sentence. At that moment in 1974, the enemy ensnared my mind, tricking me so profoundly until I stepped into the prison of my own will.

Perhaps, God left me there because He loves me.

I know that seems counterintuitive. It doesn't make sense, but it's true.

How can I come to that conclusion considering all I have experienced? Because at each brink, I now see He rescued me from drowning in my shame and circumstances. Over and over, He rescued me. He made me resilient.

It was not another person, a job, or wealth that saved me from drowning. No perfect marriage or impeccable outward appearance saved me from going under. Only God could.

It was certainly not me doing the saving, either. As hard as I tried to erase my shame through failed relationships, drinking, and drugs, and with every effort to be good, I failed at being my own rescuer. There was nothing I could do or think that would change me. Only God could.

I am also sure that His heart broke each time I turned away, believing He could not love me and going in search of another way to save myself. Perhaps, because of His love, He suffered while I roamed a winding path of destruction that ended where it began.

Nowhere on this five-decade journey have I been alone.

I believe it broke Jesus' heart to see me held down on a white chenille covered bed, legs dangling over the side while a young man violently stripped me of my voice, my power and left me with shame, fear, and trauma. I picture Him weeping at the doorway, begging with His Father to make it stop. And the Heavenly Father answers, "Don't worry. I will rescue her." I trust that Jesus waited for me on the bus when the driver sat me on his lap for his own pleasure, asking the Heavenly Father to make it stop. "Don't worry. I will rescue her," He says.

The reality is, we live in a broken world. That is not an excuse. What depraved men do to little girls is not right and never will be. But God knows every day of my life, and He knew where I would be on a summer afternoon. He planned my birth into a family with secrets and hurts. He planned to save me.

I know God loves me because I didn't die.

The day I found myself wanting to die instead of enduring another day of feeling dirty, ugly, and broken, I was drowning in shame. Seeing my abuser's face unexpectedly sent me rushing back forty years and feeling the heavy, suffocating weight of shame.

I begged God, one last time, if He was listening, let me die. The shame was too much to bear.

God was listening, and He extended His hand and hope in a whisper. "Try a counselor first," He said. The difference between hope and hopelessness and death and life depended on whether I could hear the whisper.

Wait! For there to be a conversation, there needs to be two. A relationship. Not just one person or, in this case, not just God, and not just me. For me to hear the whisper meant there was a relationship. A back and forth. Two. For me to reach out and grab God's hand meant He had to be present all along, watching and waiting to rescue me.

Swimming

I may have considered our relationship gone, but He did not. He was there watching and waiting like an earthly father watches over his children, ready to reach out a hand when they need it the most. I have seen a rescuing hand before. The image is clearly inscribed in my childhood memories, and I think of it each time I picture God reaching to rescue me.

My mother and father never took us on vacation. I am sure they spent money more appropriately on food, clothing, mortgage, and utilities. However, this one summer, they decided to take us on a trip, and they piled my brother, sister, and me in our white, wood-paneled station wagon and headed east. My grandmother, Mamaw, and her youngest son piled in with us for the trip.

That makes seven humans crammed into a vehicle. The lucky ones rode in the back where there were no seats, lying horizontally instead of sitting vertically. This was the time when seatbelts were optional. We drove more than seven hours east to Gatlinburg, Tennessee, where we vacationed in the foothills of the Great Smoky Mountains.

My brother remembers the trip better than me. He recalls that our mother bought him and my uncle a souvenir bullwhip. "It was the greatest thing I ever owned," my brother said. My sister recollects my mother buying her and me matching silver and turquoise rings. She still has hers. I, on the other hand, don't remember the ring or the bullwhip. What I do remember is the swimming pool at the motel.

We stayed in a single-level motel, where all the doors to the rooms faced the parking lot. In the center of the parking lot was a swimming pool. A pool was a great luxury for us kids. We hadn't been to a pool before that vacation that I remember. In my mind's eye, I see my mother and grandmother lounging in poolside chaises, and my father sitting alone along the side in a green folding lawn chair, leaned against the chain-link fence that encircled the pool.

In my ears, I hear the sounds of water slapping against the side of the pool while we play. What fun it was to splash and clumsily try to run in the pool. With a great "kerplop," my brother tries a belly flop. The adults chatter and whisper as they keep an eye on the kids in the shallow end of the pool. The air is hot although the sun is hidden by the towering pine trees surrounding the motel.

"Stop splashing me," I hear my brother complain.

"Stop splashing your brother," my mother warns.

The pool play ended quickly with my mother's rebuke. I bounced and bobbed in the water toward the other end of the pool, away from my complaining brother. I could hear his voice behind me, now directed at the other kids in the pool.

The next moment, there was silence.

Not aware of how a pool becomes deeper the farther you walk toward one end, I stepped off into the deep end. The water covered my head; I did not know how to swim.

Like a fly on the fence, I can see myself bobbing up and down in the water, but no one notices. I am sucking in water instead of air and trying to scream for help, but no sound comes out. My arm slaps the water's surface as if it will help me stay above the water. My thrashing looks like everyone else's pool play. I can hear my brother laughing. Does he think I am playing?

I'm going to die. I know it. I see shadows above the water as my head sinks under the water.

In slow motion, I see my father falling forward toward the pool's edge. He is stretching out his arm as far as he can.

He is yelling, "Tammy, grab my hand."

I strain to reach the edge of the pool, and my tiny hand barely grasps the tips of my father's calloused one. With one swift yank, I am out of the water. Rescued.

It's not funny, but now, decades later, we can all laugh when we talk about that memorable vacation. My brother says he remembers counting the times I disappeared under the surface of the water. "One, two…" I suppose he knew that after three dips, I was most likely gone. But I was rescued from the dreaded count of three. Others at the poolside recall that everyone except my father froze, not knowing what to do but watch.

Nearly fifty years later, I found myself in a similar situation—not at the pool physically, but emotionally. I was going under for the third time after I saw my abuser's face on social media and decided that killing myself was better than living another day in the prison of shame.

He drew me out of the water. His rescue changed everything.

Again, faithfully, Jesus reached out His hand and rescued me from certain death. He drew me out of the water. His rescue changed everything.

The Pit

I can't count the number of times Jesus rescued me, mostly from myself. Again and again, Jesus saved me from the brink, pulled me out of the pit, and set me on solid ground. He rescued me over and over, but I couldn't see it then because of the shame that clouded my vision. Now, with that lens of shame gone, I can see the many ways He rescued me.

If my father hadn't been watching me and had stayed in his chair, I would have drowned. In the same way, I did not fully comprehend what God was doing in me and around me when He rescued me from the brink. He was always watching me, and He came down to save me from my shame.

I still don't swim. Although I now have a pool with a deep end in the backyard, I never took to the water. The near-death experience left me with a lifelong fear of water. My sister and brother learned to swim and spent summers lifeguarding at the local pool. Not me. I never go in the ocean above my knees, and I never learned to swim well enough to stay alive if I needed to. I stay safely near the shallow end.

That brief moment of terror, a fleeting moment of feeling as if I would die, left me with a great fear. The fear is not about the water; it's about not being able to save myself from dying. I was in the water, thrashing and trying to scream for help, but no voice, no help came from the bobbing up and down. And I couldn't do anything about it.

I can be standing on dry land and be drowning as well. I was drowning in shame and secrets. And, metaphorically, I was going under for the last time when I cried out to God to take me because I couldn't endure another day of shame.

It wasn't the shame that was killing me so much as it was that I could not rescue myself. I needed a rescuer.

When my father pulled me from the deep end of the pool, I cried tears of fear, sobbed in gratitude that I didn't drown, and coughed up a gallon of pool water. Even a little girl knows when she has been rescued. Although a scary day, when I think about my father, that memory is only one of a few where I deeply felt my father's love for me. He was a rough, closed-off, angry man with a painful past of his own, but in that moment, I knew he loved me. He loved me so much he saved me.

My father would not let me drown. No, he was compelled to reach out for me. In the same way, my God is compelled by His love to reach out and rescue me from drowning.

So, when God reached out to save me, and I took His hand, there was a restored relationship.

The journey of returning to God has not been absent of potholes. Because the abuse and the resulting trauma and shame became part of my fiber, my mind often returns to the wounds. When I fail in some way or just plain commit sin, I reach into that proverbial "thought closet" and grab a shame coat, put it on for a few days, and wallow in self-pity.

"I am such a failure," I tell myself as I lie awake at night.

"I will never be a good Christian," I whisper under my breath.

"God has made a mistake," I finally pray.

Then, I remember. I remember how I wanted to die and God whispered in my ear. I recall how telling the secret felt. I remember how free I am. How God rescued me. I look around and see how He redeemed my life. He put all the broken pieces together and made me whole. He brought me back from the edge of despair and gave me a new song.

He did that. I did not have to.

These ups and downs come and go. Some days I need help to remember. Until I see Jesus, I will never be rid of the wounds and scars that sometimes show through. On days I can't fully recall God's saving grace, thank goodness I have multiple journals that I reread often. On their pages, I recorded God's faithfulness just for this purpose.

July 27, 2017

Father God, praise You that You never give up on me. You have pursued me all of my life.

November 10, 2018

Father God, thank You, praise You, for the revelation that what happened to me happened so that I would be here praying to You.

Among all the pages in my many black-bound journals—which I pray someone will burn when I die—I wrote a list of truths about who I am to God. I am chosen. God fearfully and wonderfully made me. I am a child of God. The more I read the list, the more I can swim when the deep water tries to take me under.

Writing this story is also how I can remember God's love for me. From the first chapter to the last word, it is God's story. The days of my life, God wrote so I could know that He loved me. That He rescued, redeemed, and restored me.

From the first chapter to the last word, it is God's story.

CHAPTER 10

Forgiven

Justice

After more than three years of visiting April regularly, my counseling
was complete. Graduation day happened weeks before the holidays
that year. I considered my graduation a Christmas miracle. I felt like
I had just been released from the hospital after a dangerous illness or
a complicated surgery that almost killed me. Every bit of me felt alive.

The twinkling Christmas lights were brighter. The holiday music
was more joyful. Freedom from shame was sweet.

If I needed more counseling, I could, of course, go back, but the
hard stuff, the deep dark places, were healing. I was ready to go out
on my own, scars and all.

There was a celebration, just me and April. She reminded me
of my state of mind and heart when I began counseling. She smiled
like a proud mother. "Look at you now."

April tasked me with marking the event. She suggested doing
something special, "Take a trip, or buy yourself a gift, a necklace or
bracelet, as a reminder of the accomplishment."

I took a trip to Paris that Christmas. The group trip was a
dream come true. I had always imagined seeing the City of Lights.

The Eiffel Tower, the Louvre, the Seine, and the cobblestone streets were not a disappointment. Sitting in tiny chairs at sidewalk cafes, I ate baskets full of decadent buttery croissants and drank gallons of the richest, darkest coffee on earth. It was wonderful.
I was healed, so it seemed.

My spiritual, emotional, and mental state were far more healthy than when I first walked through April's door. Through God's grace and buckets of blood, sweat, tears, and hundreds of tissues, I knew the truth and was learning to live the truth every day.

The abuse was not my fault. God made me. God loves me, and God forgives me. I possessed the tools to deal with dysfunctional relationships and set boundaries. My mind was pushing out the lies. I could talk about the abuse. There was no secret to hide.

But I couldn't completely let it go. My mind kept returning to the events and then reliving the fallout. I kept putting my healing, grown-up self in the place of my little-girl-self forty years ago. If the healed me were there, I would fight for the scared little girl I was. She would not have to endure what happened next. Everything would be set right.

I wanted justice.

For months after my graduation, I would let my imagination wander into dark places. The summer day my life changed forever could not be erased, but someone could pay for the sin. I concocted plans for revenge. Finding my abuser would not be too hard. He showed up on social media. I could find him again, I was sure. The statute of limitations to file charges had passed long ago. A trial forty years later would be impossible. With no legal options, I set out to take my revenge and make him pay any way possible.

My first plan was to create a secret smear campaign. I would draw up a specially-worded anonymous post and share it with the whole social media world. Those who knew him would know the truth, too.

Or I would send a letter if I could find an address. I would tell my abuser every detail of the pain he caused in my life in my letter. Every excruciating detail. It might go something along these lines:

Dear DT,

One summer day, you conjured a scheme to lure me into your home, seduce me into your mother's bedroom, and you raped me. If you don't remember, I do.

At that moment, you took away everything precious. You took my innocence, voice, and worth and left me with fear, self-hatred, and shame. You did this deed, not because I deserved it or asked for it, but because you felt like it.

I will never know if you struggled with the remorse of what you did. I believe I blocked out any memory of you in my life after that day. I don't remember seeing you on the school bus again or walking in our neighborhood, probably because I was rife with fear that you would hurt me again.

What you did was deeply wrong. You left me struggling to the point of wanting to take my life. Your moment of desire ruined any hope of believing I was loveable. I have spent my life covered in shame that belonged to you.

You hurt me too deeply to forgive.

Me

Or I would outright confront him. In my daydreams of a confrontation, I would be the judge and jury. The evidence would be presented, and he would be remorseful to the point of tears—on his knees begging my forgiveness. My response would be, "Guilty."

While I made these outrageous plans, bitterness and resentment chipped away at the confidence and peace I worked hard to find. I wasn't even aware. I found myself searching for ways to retaliate and

avenge my honor. Anger rose within me like a volcano. I deserved
justice, I told myself. The perpetrator deserved the same humiliation
and pain I endured, I insisted. With every bitter thought and fantasy
of revenge, the wound opened again.
I was going backward.

These schemes carried on for months. I flip-flopped between
healing from trauma to causing trauma. If I were building a wall, my
healing would be the foundation that crumbled with every storm and
rainy day. When the scene of the assault flashed across my mind's
eye—and it did most days—bitterness, not truth, would captivate
my thoughts, and healing thoughts fell away.

Reverse

The weather warmed, and the trees turned green again, and the memory of Paris faded. Alone in my office trying to write, my attention
wandered away, and I found myself staring out the window, letting
thoughts of the past linger too long. I picked up my phone to distract
myself from what was going through my mind. As usual, I scrolled
through social media to waste time and divert my focus. Then it
happened again. Just as jolting as the day I saw his face the first time,
there it was. My abuser's face was staring back at me—again.

This time he was dead.

His obituary popped up in my Facebook feed posted by a high
school acquaintance—someone who admired this man. He died
before I could exact my punishment.

I would never know justice.

My anger raged. "Not fair!" I screamed into my pillow. This
man's family and friends posted condolences and sentiments under
his obituary. Instead of justice and punishment, he was lauded as a

great friend and father. Bitterness bubbled and churned, threatening to erupt. The health I worked so hard to find was unraveling. Fast.

The unraveling began with a bout of tears and screaming on the inside. Screaming at God. But why, God? Why will this man not be exposed? It's not fair. I suffered shame and destruction for years, yet he receives a remembrance filled with honor. Why? Doesn't he owe me something?

The swirl of hate and venom had to stop. Before I met April and God's healing grace, I would have drunk myself into a pity prison, or worse, considered ending my life. Once again, I needed to hear God's whisper.

My anger pushed out any voice but my plea for setting things right. Whatever I chose to do from here, it was clear this justice quest was at an end, at least here on earth. I would have to let go of that pursuit. Justice was not mine to exact anyway.

Now I had to make a choice. I could stay on the road paved with bitterness and anger and shrouded in darkness. On this route, every step added interest and taxes to the already unrecoverable debt left by my abuser. And I knew he could never ever pay off what I felt he owed. If I stayed this course, the cost would be the healing I had enjoyed for the first time. Or I could take another path.

I could give the gift I received.

One of the most difficult gifts to give is forgiveness. We want it from others and are incredibly grateful for the forgiveness from God. However, we are slow to offer forgiveness to those who inflict harm.

I'm not talking about the kind of harm from unkind words spoken in anger or the injury experienced when the party invitation does not come. No, I mean the harm that slaps you across the face when you think about how it happened. The abuse, the physical pain, and the emotional anguish that lingers day in and day out. The harm that leaves you curled up in the fetal position when the shame ties you in knots. I'm talking about the kind of harm that changes you from the inside out—that kind of damage.

Forgiving that kind of harm feels impossible. How could I? This boy took my voice, my innocence, and changed who I could have been. Forever. Then, a grown man who knew better took advantage of a powerless, voiceless little girl. From that time forward, my view of love and affection would be dysfunctional. How would forgiveness ever make that right again? What about the decades of shame and the destruction created along the way? How could forgiveness make a difference?

But giving forgiveness gifts the giver more than the receiver.

But giving forgiveness gifts the giver more than the receiver.

I considered my debt, the debt I owed God. My healing journey started with thoughts of suicide. Layers of shame and guilt brought me to that place, mostly because I carried shame belonging to someone else. I lugged around the shame of my bad choices and the guilt of a sin-filled life that was too heavy to bear. This burden of shame, guilt, and sins I believed not even God could forgive. It was a deep debt I could never repay, but God canceled my debt because of what Jesus did.

Although I trusted that God's forgiveness includes me, I'm not sure I fully understood what it means to forgive someone who caused me harm. At that point, my vision was clouded by bitterness, anger, and resentment.

The most common definition of forgiveness is "the cancelation of a debt." I imagined my credit card company sending me a letter that says, "Your account is closed, and your debt is canceled. Have a nice day." Does forgiveness work that way?

Real forgiveness, healing forgiveness, does.

"Healing is linked to forgiveness." Corrie Ten Boom wrote these words about forgiveness after she survived the horrors of a Nazi concentration camp.[1] She traveled the world after World War II, teaching and speaking about forgiveness. The world was agonizing and distraught over the deep division caused by the war. She implored others to forgive. Forgiveness was necessary to move on and live whole again.

During a speaking engagement in Germany, she came face-to-face with one of the brutal guards from Ravensbrück, where she suffered heartbreaking abuse and the loss of her beloved sister. As Corrie finished a speech about God's forgiveness, the guard, now a Christian, approached Corrie. She recognized him even before he stretched out his hand toward her. Changed by grace and salvation, the guard asked one impossible question. "Will you forgive me?" he asked.

How could she? The story goes that Corrie paused for what seemed like hours before she responded. Although it was only a few moments, Corrie uttered the words that led her to complete healing. "I forgive you."

Forgiveness changed everything.

I was learning that forgiveness is not a feeling like anger and happiness. It is not an emotion you find in circumstances and people. It is a choice. It is action. To reach the end—well, almost the end—of the healing journey, I needed to understand that I was forgiven, and in turn, I needed to forgive. On my strength, I could do neither.

To know true healing, to live unbound by the past, I first had to understand without a doubt that God did forgive me. He is God enough to forgive what I did in those forty-plus years. Once and for all, I am forgiven. My heart needed to grasp that reality. Then, I had to forgive those who abused me and left me believing I was shameful, unlovable, and unwanted. Without the first step, I could not take the second step. Without the second step, I would sink back into the prison, this time chained by bitterness and rage. I had to cancel the debt.

Mountaintop

I have this vision of debt-canceling forgiveness and the opposite, which is unforgiveness. The picture in my imagination of forgiveness looks like a mountain. The terrain of the mountain is rugged and covered with rocks and boulders. At the base of the mountain, darkness hides the sight of the summit. Clouds hinder the view. Between the base and the apex, the terrain is treacherous and unstable. But a climber knows that the terrain is beautiful and bright at the top of the mountain, lit by the sun with a front row seat and a view of the stars. Climbers strain toward the top.

To reach the top, a climber must traverse the difficult terrain before her. Each step is a struggle made more difficult by the ropes tied around her ankles and arms. The ropes are tied to the climber by the bitterness and anger from unforgiveness. She can take steps, but the ropes keep pulling her backward. Shame and guilt help bitterness and rage take hold of the climber. But what if the climber could cut the ropes and be free to reach the summit?

The only way to cut the ties is forgiveness. It did not feel right, and I did not want to consider it as an answer, but it was the only way to be truly free and reach the summit.

I spent the time and hard heart work to process the trauma. Now I had to make another choice. Was I going to stop where I was on my healing journey and allow unforgiveness to take hold and steal my freedom, or would I take another giant step toward healing and reach the mountaintop? The choice is obvious now. I had to choose forgiveness.

Forgiving was almost as hard as telling the secret.

Forgiving was almost as hard as telling the secret.

Fortunately, I am not required to muster up a big helping of forgiveness. It doesn't work that way. The only possible way I could forgive this most profound harm was to look at the forgiveness I received for the deepest harm I inflicted on God. For all of the sin I trudged through for decades, He forgave me. I know because He says so. And I, therefore, cannot withhold what God pours out.

Instead of a letter throwing blame and bitter poison, I wrote a final note.

Dear DT,

I'm not sure where your soul finds you, but I pray it finds rest in Jesus. I don't know what happened to you after the last time you crossed my path, but I hope you found relief. I suspect you had your own pain that led you to do what you did to me on a summer afternoon.

At first, I wanted you to suffer as much as I. What you did was wrong and evil. Now I find myself offering what I needed most before I found healing from the pain you gave me—grace and forgiveness. May God have mercy on you as He has shown me mercy.

Me

I folded the letter, tore it into small pieces, and set it aflame. I watched as it turned to ashes. Beauty for ashes.

So, I cut him loose. I canceled the debt. And I have to continue to wake up each day and cut the ties of unforgiveness. I must choose forgiveness each time I feel bitterness and an ache for justice begin in my head. I choose forgiveness before the ache reaches my heart.

In the same way, I must continue to retrain my thinking to know that I am loved, wanted, and valuable. I must forgive. I have to remind myself of the forgiveness I have received every day. So much forgiveness. Out of that abundance, I must offer forgiveness to the one who harmed me the most. If I do not, I start at the base of the mountain again.

What was meant for harm, God used for good.

That does not mean what he did is excused—far from it. What happened was illegal and immoral. What happened was rape. What happened was sexual assault. There is no way to whitewash the facts. But forgiveness means the consequences of those facts do not bind me. He and the evil he intended have lost their power over me. I have a voice and a choice. What was meant for harm, God used for good.

Step by heavy step, forgiveness unbound me from the ropes that hindered my journey to the summit. The terrain upward was never wholly cleared of obstacles. There were days I experienced a trigger that sent my mind and heart spiraling toward the bottom again. But without the ropes of unforgiveness and bitterness holding me back, I could get up and head to the mountaintop again, each time stronger than before.

The elusive top of the mountain is in the distance. When I reach the top, I will see all around in every direction. I imagine looking below me and seeing the rocks and stones I carried in the pockets of my coat of shame. I leave them where they lie. I am rescued from that weight. I look up, and in one direction, I see a future without shame and regret. I gaze at the healing path I see far away winding through the valley. In another direction, I see how my Heavenly Father redeemed every moment of suffering. Nothing was wasted.

He used every ounce to shape me and strengthen me so I could stand here—at the top.

And above me, I see a glimpse of eternity where I will never feel the pain of shame and secrets and will be complete, finished, and forever healed.

Not the End

This is not the end of the story. This is not the finish line. I wish it were.

There is still work to be done. When I finally let go of my abuse secret, I believed life would be easy and free. I do know freedom and loving, and living is easier without shame. But pain and fear still haunt my heart. What happened to me as a little girl in the summer of 1974 cannot be changed. No amount of time or words will erase this reality. So, healing is ongoing. Through God's grace every day, I work to lessen its effect on my heart, mind, and soul.

Nothing would be sweeter than to know that I would never struggle another day with thoughts of no self-worth or of not being loved. But I do. I also dream of going one day without thinking about the past. But I still do. Complete healing is in my future home in heaven. In the meantime, between here and there, there is much work to be done.

There is work to be done to transform our world into one where there is no sexual abuse, secrets, or shame. Women continue to hide their secret and drown in shame. Women still suffer the pain of abuse. Until that is not true, there is more work to be done.

There is work to be done to help women still holding onto secrets and shame. Since beginning this journey, every time I speak about abuse, secrets, and shame, I meet women with a similar story. Our stories vary a little in the details, but the shame, fear, and pain are the same. These women keep their secrets and carry shame just like I did. They want to tell, but they fear. They want freedom from shame. They want hope and healing. They want to be rescued. And they need a safe person, a safe place, to tell their story and begin their healing journey.

If you are one of these women, I urge you to find help and a compassionate place to share your secret. Take the first step. And don't give up if the first person you tell is not the right person. Someone is waiting to hear your precious story. You can tell. You can find healing. You are stronger than you think you are. Tell your story, uncover your secret, and be rescued.

Someone is waiting to hear your precious story.

There is work for healing women like me. Women who know freedom from their secret possess the gift hurting women need. One in six women will know or have known the pain of sexual abuse, and the majority of those women never tell. Healing women heal women. Our stories show how ordinary women with ordinary strength find extraordinary healing. Our stories give hope.

Hope.

They see in us that what was meant for evil, God uses for good. What was meant for harm and control, God uses to rescue. The work we have to do is to be that safe, compassionate place where women tell their story. It's an honor to receive their precious stories and hold their hands. Through us, God can bring hope and healing. God can bring freedom. God can rescue.

Yes, there is much work to be done.

Reader
Guide

Chapter 1: Forty Years Later

1. In Chapter 1, I write about how I made big plans to end my pain, and *then* I went to God for His approval or help. He answered my prayer in an unexpected way. Where do you go first with hard problems? Do you turn to friends and family? Or do you hide and withdraw, hoping no one notices? What do you think might happen if you went to God first?

2. When God answered my prayer with, "Try counseling," I could
    have disobeyed. Before that day, I often did. But because I obeyed,
    He blessed me abundantly with hope and healing. Our tendency
    is to ignore God's directions if they are too hard or not what we
    want. Where do you need to obey God?

    _____

    _____

    _____

    _____

    _____

    _____

    _____

    _____

    _____

    _____

    _____

    _____

    _____

    _____

    _____

    _____

3. Because of shame and secrets, I felt I had no worth or value.
   I looked for my value in people and what I could do or didn't
   do. The truth is, our value is determined by God, and He says
   we are a masterpiece. Think about what makes you feel like a
   treasure. Is it people? Or what you have accomplished? Where
   do you find worth?

_____

_____

_____

_____

_____

_____

_____

_____

_____

_____

_____

_____

_____

_____

_____

4. Studies show that everyone has more than ten secrets they have never told anyone, mostly because they are afraid of what people would think. We hide our secrets in shame. But God know everything about us. What secret(s) do you hide? Do you think God sees you differently because of your secret(s)?

_____

_____

_____

_____

_____

_____

_____

_____

_____

_____

_____

_____

_____

_____

_____

5. One thing that helps us grasp the truth that God is always
    watching over us, that He is present in every circumstance, is
    meditating on Scripture. As you meditate on the following
    Scripture, think about the comfort that comes from experiencing
    God's presence right where you are no matter what has happened
    to you or because of what you have done. He sees you, knows
    you and is always present and ready to rescue you.

    > *"Don't be afraid of those who want to kill your body; they*
    > *cannot touch your soul. Fear only God, who can destroy*
    > *both soul and body in hell. What is the price of two*
    > *sparrows—one copper coin? But not a single sparrow*
    > *can fall to the ground without your Father knowing it.*
    > *And the very hairs on your head are all numbered. So*
    > *don't be afraid; you are more valuable to God than a*
    > *whole flock of sparrows."* (Matthew 10:28-31)

    What thoughts come to mind when you read and meditate on
    these words? What comfort do you have to know that God sees
    you, no matter where you are?

    _____

    _____

    _____

    _____

    _____

    _____

    _____

Chapter 2: Origin Story

1. It is clear that our origins affect how we live and how we see ourselves. For me, my family of origin, without intent, left me needing affirmation and affection, and I felt responsible for my mother and father. How has where you come from affected how you see yourself?

_____

_____

_____

_____

_____

_____

_____

_____

_____

_____

_____

_____

_____

_____

_____

_____

2. As I share in Chapter 2, my grandmother was responsible for
    introducing me to Jesus by taking me to church with her on
    Sundays. Who introduced you to Jesus? Who can you introduce
    Jesus to? If you do not know Jesus, He knows you and is waiting
    to rescue you. Please ask someone to introduce you.

_____

_____

_____

_____

_____

_____

_____

_____

_____

_____

_____

_____

_____

_____

_____

_____

3. My counselor used a personal timeline to help me process and
    understand how events in my life altered and shaped me. Consider
    making a timeline listing all the events you can remember and
    the dates in one column. In the second column, write how you
    felt about that event. Are there events or things you experienced
    that you have never told a single person?

    _____

    _____

    _____

    _____

    _____

    _____

    _____

    _____

    _____

    _____

    _____

    _____

    _____

    _____

    _____

4. Before you were born into your family, God knew you, and He
    also knows every day of your life. Where you came from and the
    events of your life are not by accident. Meditate on the following
    Scripture that reminds us that God knows us best.

> *For you created my inmost being;*
>   *you knit me together in my mother's womb.*
> *I praise you because I am fearfully and wonderfully made;*
>   *your works are wonderful,*
>   *I know that full well.*
> *My frame was not hidden from you*
>   *when I was made in the secret place,*
>   *when I was woven together in the depths of the earth.*
> *Your eyes saw my unformed body;*
>   *all the days ordained for me were written in your book*
>   *before one of them came to be.*
> *How precious to me are your thoughts, God!*
>   *How vast is the sum of them!*
> *Were I to count them,*
>   *they would outnumber the grains of sand—*
>   *when I awake, I am still with you.*
> (Psalm 138:13-18)

What gives you the most comfort from this passage?

_____

_____

_____

_____

_____

_____

Chapter 3: Fallout

1. There are consequences for every action—even things that happen
   in secret. No one except me and the neighbor boy knew what
   happened, yet the ripple of consequences lasts today. Can you
   remember an event that seemed inconsequential, yet you can
   see the consequences today? How does the event compare to
   the consequences?

_____

_____

_____

_____

_____

_____

_____

_____

_____

_____

_____

_____

_____

_____

2. An important part of healing from any trauma or hurt is replacing
   old thoughts with truth. As I described in Chapter 3, I believed
   many lies about myself. I even blamed myself for what happened.
   Not true. What lies are you believing about yourself? What truths
   can replace these lies?

_____

_____

_____

_____

_____

_____

_____

_____

_____

_____

_____

_____

_____

_____

3. In Chapter 3, I mention how secrets cannot live in the light. Once
    they are exposed to light, they shrivel and die. They are no longer
    secret. Light dispels darkness. And the secret does not have to
    be about something that happened. It can be unresolved hurt
    and pain. Are you hiding something that needs to be exposed
    to light? What is hidden that needs to be revealed? Even sharing
    your secret hurt and pain with Jesus shines light on the darkness.

_____

_____

_____

_____

_____

_____

_____

_____

_____

_____

_____

_____

_____

_____

4. Fear grips everyone. For me, it was a fear of being in a small space unable to escape. It can also be a fear of not being loved or wanted. Fear is the fallout of hurt and pain. What if we could remember that we are never alone, that God is with us all the time? Meditate today on what God says about fear.

> *"Don't be afraid, for I am with you. Don't be discouraged, for I am your God. I will strengthen you and help you. I will hold you up with my victorious right hand."*
> (Isaiah 41:10)

_____

_____

_____

_____

_____

_____

_____

_____

_____

_____

_____

_____

_____

Chapter 4: Running Away

1. Think about those Bible saints who ran away from circumstances: Moses, Jonah, Elisha. Even God's great followers ran from consequences or His commands. Running away is sometimes our first reaction. Think about your past experience with difficult circumstances. Did you run away from any? How did running help or hurt the situation?

_____

_____

_____

_____

_____

_____

_____

_____

_____

_____

_____

_____

_____

_____

2. When I returned home after living in New York for a few years, I
    felt like the prodigal daughter. Prodigal means to waste resources.
    The son in Luke 15:11-32 left home, squandered the resources
    he possessed, and was left with nothing. His only hope was to
    return to where he came from. Have you ever wasted resources
    such as love, respect, and admiration? Looking back, what would
    you do differently? How can you nurture these resources instead
    of wasting them?

_____

_____

_____

_____

_____

_____

_____

_____

_____

_____

_____

_____

3. Shame is universal. Everyone will suffer from shame at some point. Physically, shame is described as a burning sensation in the chest or on the face, a feeling of being exposed. The response to shame, however, is individual. The pain of shame for me manifested in running away from what caused the shame, which ended up causing more shame. How does shame show up in your life? Do you run, hide, or try to deny or blame others for shame?

_____

_____

_____

_____

_____

_____

_____

_____

_____

_____

_____

_____

_____

_____

4. Shame says, "Something is wrong with me." This is a lie. God is perfect and holy. God created us. And if He made us, then we are perfectly made. Today, begin to dispel the lie that something is not right about you. You are perfectly made and continually being made perfect. Meditate on the following truth.

    For we are God's masterpiece. *He has created us anew in Christ Jesus, so we can do the good things he planned for us long ago.* (Ephesians 2:10, emphasis mine)

    How can you replace the lie that says something is wrong with the truth that says you are a masterpiece?

    _____

    _____

    _____

    _____

    _____

    _____

    _____

    _____

    _____

    _____

    _____

Chapter 5: Survival

1. A survivor is someone who "...survives; specifically a person who has survived an ordeal or great misfortune."[1] Most people have survived something: a great loss, the death of a loved one, an unexpected trauma. What ordeal or misfortune have you survived? Do you consider yourself a survivor?

_____

_____

_____

_____

_____

_____

_____

_____

_____

_____

_____

_____

_____

2. Resiliency is an attribute of survivors. It is the ability to endure
    and grow through a difficult situation or event. Being resilient
    has been described as climbing a mountain with a trail map.
    Climbing requires time and help. Think about difficult times
    and situations that you have endured. What did you learn about
    yourself? About God?

_____

_____

_____

_____

_____

_____

_____

_____

_____

_____

_____

_____

_____

_____

3. One of the many things I learned about God through this journey is that He fights for us. We are never to endure or battle circumstances alone. Scripture says He is our Mighty Warrior. Today, meditate on the following Scripture. Eternalize this truth and remember that God always fights for you. You never have to run away from your circumstances because He is there to fight for you.

    > *The Lord your God is with you,*
    >   *the Mighty Warrior who saves.*
    > *He will take great delight in you;*
    >   *in his love he will no longer rebuke you,*
    >   *but will rejoice over you with singing.*
    > (Zephaniah 3:17)

    How does it feel to know that God Himself will rejoice over you with singing?

    _____

    _____

    _____

    _____

    _____

    _____

    _____

    _____

    _____

    _____

    _____

Chapter 6: Secret Sickness

1. In Chapter 6, I explain how the trauma of abuse left me feeling like a black sheep, the one no one wanted. That is not what God says about us. He says we are chosen (John 15:16). We are His very own possession (1 Peter 2:9). Have you ever felt as if you did not belong? Have you ever felt there was something different about you? If so, how does knowing you are chosen by God change that perspective?

_____

_____

_____

_____

_____

_____

_____

_____

_____

_____

_____

_____

_____

_____

_____

2. Over ninety percent of what we worry about happening does not
    happen. "What ifs" crowd our thinking and give us great anxiety.
    But Scripture tells us to cast our fears, worries, and anxieties
    on God because He cares (1 Peter 5:7). What is your worst fear,
    worry, or concern? What is your worst nightmare? Can you share
    that fear with God?

_____

_____

_____

_____

_____

_____

_____

_____

_____

_____

_____

_____

_____

3. The moments when we overwhelmingly experience the presence of Jesus, like the day He was present as I knelt next to my red ice chest, remind us that we are His, that He sees us, and that He hears our prayers. Describe a time that you knew Jesus was near. How did He answer your prayer?

---

4. Sometimes it can feel like God does not hear our prayers. We begin to think that He is saying, "I'm not listening." That is not so. He hears His children and answers. Perhaps not in a way we expected or imagined, but He hears our pleas. As you meditate on the following Scripture, consider the prayers you gave up on asking for. Then think about how Jesus tells us to pray.

> *"Keep on asking, and you will receive what you ask for. Keep on seeking, and you will find. Keep on knocking, and the door will be opened to you. For everyone who asks, receives. Everyone who seeks, finds. And to everyone who knocks, the door will be opened."* *(Matthew 7:7-8)*

What request do you need to pray persistently?

_____

_____

_____

_____

_____

_____

_____

_____

_____

Chapter 7: New Vision

1. For so many years my secret and shame held me captive. I could even describe the imaginary cage within a prison with only a fraction of light seeping through. What secret and shame hold you captive? It does not have to be abuse and the fallout. Perhaps, it's a terrible hurt or pain, or a huge disappointment or loss. What keeps you from living free?

_____

_____

_____

_____

_____

_____

_____

_____

_____

_____

_____

_____

2. I learned that the key to my freedom was telling the secret. Once I told my counselor the secret, I was free. Each time I told my story, my burden was lighter. It seems difficult, probably impossible, but who might you tell your secret to? What do you expect to happen if you tell your story?

_____

_____

_____

_____

_____

_____

_____

_____

_____

_____

_____

_____

_____

_____

_____

_____

_____

3. For a time, I doubted whether God was with me during the decades before I encountered Jesus in the kitchen of our rental house, but there was so much evidence that was not true. Looking back on your life, can you see where God protected you? Maybe you survived a life-threatening situation, or something you thought would happen did not. What evidence do you have that God was present?

_____

_____

_____

_____

_____

_____

_____

_____

_____

_____

_____

_____

_____

4. For so long I believed that if I ran from God, He would not know
    my secret and that He didn't have time for me anyway. Scripture
    tells something altogether different. God knows everything about
    us. He knows our coming and going. He knows our thoughts
    and plans, desires and needs. He knows the very number of hairs
    on our head. We have no secrets with God. Today, consider the
    following passage and how God knows everything about you
    and yet never turns away.

> *O Lord, you have examined my heart*
> *and know everything about me.*
> *You know when I sit down or stand up.*
> *You know my thoughts even when I'm far away.*
> *You see me when I travel*
> *and when I rest at home.*
> *You know everything I do.*
> *You know what I am going to say*
> *even before I say it, Lord.*
> *You go before me and follow me.*
> *You place your hand of blessing on my head.*
> *Such knowledge is too wonderful for me,*
> *too great for me to understand!*
> (Psalm 139:1-6)

What comfort do you experience being aware that God knows
everything about you? Nothing is hidden.

_____

_____

_____

_____

_____

Chapter 8: Telling

1. In this chapter, I share about my "thought closet." Years of listening to lies the enemy planted in my mind left me with thoughts that needed to be "ridded out." What is in your thought closet? What negative thoughts and lies does the enemy try to make you believe that you need to exchange for the truth?

_____

_____

_____

_____

_____

_____

_____

_____

_____

_____

_____

_____

_____

_____

_____

2. In Chapter 8, I write, "The difficulty exists where the enemy lives—in my mind—and his battle plan is to attack when I am down." Being prepared for battle is key to winning the war. Do you notice that the enemy attacks when you are weak or struggling? What lies does the enemy use in his attack?

_____

_____

_____

_____

_____

_____

_____

_____

_____

_____

_____

_____

_____

_____

3. Recognizing negative thoughts is the first step to cleaning out your "thought closet." Replacing those thoughts with the truth is the next step. My counselor urged me to repeat, "Nothing is wrong with me," loud and proud. Then, each time I began to slide toward false thoughts, I would repeat these words over and over until the lie was replaced. What truths about yourself can you repeat loud and proud? What true phrase about who you are in Christ can you repeat over and over until it pushes out the lies of the enemy?

_____

_____

_____

_____

_____

_____

_____

_____

_____

_____

_____

_____

4. There is a war, and the battlefield is our minds. We need a strategy
    and weapons to defeat the invisible enemy, and our Heavenly
    Father, a Mighty Warrior, gives us what we need to fight. Today,
    put on your armor and attack the lies. Meditate on the following
    Scripture that reminds us that we are equipped to do battle.

    > *Put on all of God's armor so that you will be able to*
    > *stand firm against all strategies of the devil. For we*
    > *are not fighting against flesh-and-blood enemies, but*
    > *against evil rulers and authorities of the unseen world,*
    > *against mighty powers in this dark world, and against*
    > *evil spirits in the heavenly places. Therefore, put on*
    > *every piece of God's armor so you will be able to resist*
    > *the enemy in the time of evil. Then after the battle*
    > *you will still be standing firm.* (Ephesians 6:11-13)

    After you read this passage, are you ready for battle? How will
    you fight the enemy?

    _____

    _____

    _____

    _____

    _____

    _____

    _____

    _____

    _____

Chapter 9: Rescued

1. We are not promised a life free of trials. According to Scripture, we should count our trials as blessings. When we do, God turns our weakness and pain into strength and comfort. Of course, I would rather have a fairytale story like I describe in Chapter 9, but God has used the story He gave me for good. What trials and difficulties have you experienced that seemed too difficult to endure? How do you think God can use those difficulties for good?

_____

_____

_____

_____

_____

_____

_____

_____

_____

_____

_____

_____

2. The shame of abuse stood between me and God. I believed that
    He could not love me because I was shameful. This is not true
    and a BIG lie of the enemy. God loves us and chose us even
    while we were sinners (Romans 5:8). What do you think stands
    between you and God?

_____

_____

_____

_____

_____

_____

_____

_____

_____

_____

_____

_____

_____

_____

3. Sometimes God feels far away. The truth is He never moves. We run and hide from Him because we feel unworthy and unlovable. Are you hiding or running from God? Does He seem distant? If so, what makes you want to run and hide? Do you know that God is waiting for you to return to Him?

_____

_____

_____

_____

_____

_____

_____

_____

_____

_____

_____

_____

_____

_____

4. In Chapter 9, I describe how my earthly father rescued me from drowning. In my mind, I can clearly see him, with one hand, lift me out of the water and into safety. To me, this is a visual of how God lifted me out of the pit of shame and secrets and into the light. Today, consider the following Scripture about how God rescues you.

> *He sent from on high, he took me;*
> *he drew me out of many waters.*
> *He rescued me from my strong enemy*
> *and from those who hated me,*
> *for they were too mighty for me.*
> *They confronted me in the day of my calamity,*
> *but the Lord was my support.*
> *He brought me out into a broad place;*
> *he rescued me, because he delighted in me.*
> (Psalm 18:16-19, ESV)

In the last verse of this passage, it says God rescues you because *He delights in you.* How does this change the way you view how God saves you from your secrets and shame?

_____

_____

_____

_____

_____

_____

_____

Chapter 10: Forgiven

1. After I learned and lived the truth that the abuse was not my fault and the shame belonged to my abuser, I wanted justice. I wanted him to suffer the same pain I had for so many years. This is natural. We want equalization. An eye for an eye. Have you ever wanted justice for a wrong? What did you want the other person to do or suffer? Do you think your form of justice would erase the wrong? What if you received earthly justice for your wrongs?

_____

_____

_____

_____

_____

_____

_____

_____

_____

_____

_____

_____

_____

2. I would never face my abuser or those who wronged me, and
    bitterness began to grow and kill the healing I celebrated. Justice
    is ultimately God's. The answer to my bitterness was to forgive
    someone I would never see again, and I would repeat this for-
    giveness every time bitterness sprouted. Who do you need to
    forgive and why? Would you rather seethe in bitterness or live
    in the freedom that comes from forgiveness?

_____

_____

_____

_____

_____

_____

_____

_____

_____

_____

_____

_____

_____

3. Celebrating milestones is important in making progress. When I "graduated" from counseling, I marked the milestone by taking a trip. And the milestone does not have to be the end of three years of counseling. The event can be the day you told your secret, or the moment you realized that shame does not hold you captive. And the celebrate does not have to include a ten-hour plane ride. The important thing is to mark the moment. What event do you have to celebrate? How will you mark the day?

_____

_____

_____

_____

_____

_____

_____

_____

_____

_____

_____

_____

_____

_____

4. When we remember that we have been forgiven by our holy and perfect God, it is easier to forgive others for even the worst. We are commanded to forgive as we have been forgiven. This means forgiving ourselves as well. Meditate on and memorize the following Scripture. Consider the distance of your sin from the One who forgave.

> *The Lord is compassionate and merciful,*
>   *slow to get angry and filled with unfailing love.*
> *He will not constantly accuse us,*
>   *nor remain angry forever.*
> *He does not punish us for all our sins;*
>   *he does not deal harshly with us, as we deserve.*
> *For his unfailing love toward those who fear him*
>   *is as great as the height of the heavens above the earth.*
> *He has removed our sins as far from us*
>   *as the east is from the west.*
> (Psalm 103:8-12)

How does the freedom from secrets, shame, and sin change the way we live?

_____

_____

_____

_____

_____

_____

_____

Notes

Introduction: Why Tell the Story?

1. "Victims of Sexual Violence: Statistics," RAINN, accessed March 1, 2021, https://www.rainn.org/statistics/victims-sexual-violence.

Chapter 2

1. Harper Lee, *To Kill a Mockingbird*, (New York: J. B. Lippincott & Co., 1960), 256.

Chapter 3

1. Bessel Van Der Kolk, *The Body Keeps the Score: Brain, Mind, and Body in the Healing of Trauma* (New York: Penguin Books, 2015), 21.

2. Ibid, 21.

3. "Victims of Sexual Violence: Statistics," RAINN, accessed March 1, 2021, https://www.rainn.org/statistics/victims-sexual-violence.

Chapter 4

1. Brené Brown, *I Thought It Was Just Me (but it isn't): Making the Journey from "What Will People Think?" to "I Am Enough"* (New York: Gotham Books, 2007), 5.

Chapter 5

1. "Survivor," Dictionary.com, accessed March 31, 2021, https://www.dictionary.com/browse/survivor.

Chapter 6

1. "Truism," Cambridge Dictionary, accessed April 7, 2021, https://dictionary.cambridge.org/us/dictionary/english/truism

2. "Black Sheep," Collins Dictionary, accessed April 8, 2021, https://www.collinsdictionary.com/us/dictionary/english-thesaurus/black-sheep#black-sheep__1

3.   Dan B. Allender, *The Wounded Heart: Hope for Adult Victims of Childhood Sexual Abuse* (Colorado Springs, CO: NavPress, 1990), 122.

4.   "Wreckage," YourDictionary.com, accessed April 7, 2021, https://www.yourdictionary.com/wreckage.

Chapter 8

1.   *Call the Midwife*, season 9, episode 7, directed by Syd Macartney, written by Heide Thomas, aired May 10, 2020, BBC, https://www.bbc.co.uk/programmes/m000fk24.

2.   Jennifer Rothschild, *Me, Myself, and Lies: What to Say When You Talk to Yourself* (Eugene, Oregon: Harvest House Publishers, 2007), 25.

Chapter 10

1.   Eric Metaxas, "The Test of Forgiveness: Corrie ten Boom," Faith Gateway, accessed March 1, 2021, https://www.faithgateway.com/forgiveness-corrie-ten-boom/#.YG5cca9KiUk.

Reader Guide

1.   "Survivor." YourDictionary.com, accessed April 7, 2021, https://www.yourdictionary.com/survivor.

Acknowledgments:
My Deepest Gratitude

There are so many family members, friends, and people who have helped me make the dream of a book come true. The list itself could be made into a book. And I am convinced it is possible there are not enough words to convey how grateful I am for their presence in my life. However, I will try.

This is not my story, but God's. There was a time I prayed He would take it from me. I begged Him to remove this thorn. Gratefully, He did not, and now I am overflowing with gratitude that He gave me the endurance and the ability to put His story of my life on the pages of this book.

My family deserves a whole ocean of gratitude and acknowledgement. They are the threads woven through the tapestry of my story. I pray my sister and brother know they were used by God in His rescue plan. My sister-in-law and my brother-in-law play major roles as well. They could have dismissed me, but instead joined in the journey. I am grateful to my mother and father for giving me all they had and then some. I love you all so much.

To my sons, Ian, Kyle, and Ryan, you are the reason I did not give up and drown in a sea of shame. You are precious gifts that I never deserved. You are the earthly vision of unconditional love and acceptance. Even at my worst, you loved me. Thank you. And thank you for the beautiful daughters-in-law you share with me. You are all the most precious jewels in my crown to come.

My husband would sheepishly say he had nothing to do with the completion of this dream, but he would be wrong. He is the one who nudged me to pursue a degree, quit full-time work, and focus on school and writing. He makes this dream possible. Without his support and urging, I would not be a writer.

There are so many friends for whom I am thankful that I will not try to name them all because I am afraid I will leave someone out. There are church friends, writer friends, and even online friends who I want to thank. I met some of you at writing conferences and some through groups on social media. I found so many of you when God blessed that our paths would cross. Your support and encouragement are bricks on which this dream is built.

All of this would not be possible without the compassionate help of my earthly counselor, "April." It was not a happy accident that God led me to her office. He specially designed her for this task. Her tender care and encouragement were the salve and balm my heart needed to begin healing. Her office is where I left many emotional rocks and cried rivers of tears. Thank you, April, for being the guide to my healing journey. (And I'm sorry for using so many tissues!)

My dear dream defender and writing coach, Renee Fisher, must be credited with making this dream come true. She has turned me away from the delete key more than once. Most of all, God gave her the ability to see something in me I could not see. She helped peel away the layers of my insecurity and under the surface found the story I was meant to write, not the one I thought I was supposed to write. Thank you, Renee. I pray we have a lifelong friendship and bring many dreams to life.

I am also grateful for those who made this story into a book. Thank you, Rebekah Benham, for making my writing better, correct, and more interesting to read. And, thank you, Nelly Murariu, for creating the perfect wrapper for these pages.

And I must thank you, my reader. Every book needs great readers. You make the dream complete.

About the Author

Tamela Turbeville is a trauma survivor healed by grace. She writes so that women who suffered similar trauma, a prodigal past or live with painful secrets know they are loved and wanted. They are His beautiful masterpiece. Tamela's hope is that by telling her story and speaking about her journey, other hurting women see they too can cut the chains of shame and begin their personal healing journey. She works from her home in the woods where she finds it easier to write when surrounded by her six rescue dogs.

Connect at **livingoneword.com** and **tamelaturbeville.com**.